The Traybake & Sheet Cake Recipe Book

The best easy, tried and tested recipes all baked in a traybake tin

Barbara Glebska

THE TRAYBAKE & SHEET CAKE RECIPE BOOK
The best easy, tried and tested recipes all baked in a traybake tin

First Edition 2022

Copyright©2022Barbara Glebska
Photographs Copyright©2022Barbara Glebska
www.harrowphotographer.co.uk

No part of this publication may be reproduced, stored in a retrieval system or transmitted, in any form or by any means, electronic, mechanical, photocopying, recording or otherwise, without the prior written permission of the copyright holder.

CONTENTS

Amaretti Crunch Cake
Apricot and Marzipan Cake
Baked Cheesecake
Banana and Pineapple Cake
Berry and Coconut Slices
Caramel and Pear Cake
Choc Chip Slices
Chocolate Meringue Traybake
Coconut Chocolate Slices
Double Chocolate and Nut Brownie
Easter Slices
Fruit Crumble Sponge
Fruit Curd Bars
Fudgy Coffee and Nut Shortbread
Ginger Flapjack Bars
Lemon Honey and Polenta Cake
Meringue, Almond and Blackberry Cake
Millionaires Shortbread
Peanut and Fudge Brownies
Peanut Butter Cake
Pineapple Upside-Down Cake
Raspberry Mousse Slices
Sticky Apple Traybake
Stollen Squares
Summer Fruit Slices
Tiramisu
Toffee and Apple Flapjack Squares
Vanilla Sponge
White Chocolate and Pecan Blondies
Whole Orange Cake

Hints and Tips

It is recommended using a digital scale for exact weight measurements which will result in consistent results and perfect cakes.

If you decide to use the cups volume method, fill the cup with the ingredient, then, scrape a knife across the top of the measuring cup to level the top.

• It is very important to follow the recipe at each stage and keep to the right oven temperatures. A few of the recipes ask that the temperature is lowered during baking, this ensures the cake is baked in the centre and doesn't sink.

• Set the oven rack to the middle of the oven

• Don't open the oven during the first 20 minutes of baking as the change in oven temperature might cause the cake to sink

• All the cakes are fully baked when a wooden skewer inserted into the middle of the cake comes out clean.

• Before starting a recipe prepare the tin and pre heat the oven.

• Have all the ingredients ready to hand.

• The cakes taste better the following day once completely cooled.

• The best way to line the tin is using parchment paper. This does not need any greasing. Line the tin with a strip of the paper with the ends overhanging the long sides of the tin. Loosen the end sides of the loaf cake with a knife when the cake is ready for taking out of the tin and pull up using the paper.

Tin size
All the recipes are calculated for an inside measurement
7 inches x 11 inches (18cmx28cm) traybake tin

Equipment
Traybake tin (preferably loose bottom)
Kitchen scales
Mixing bowl/s
Electric hand whisk or mixer
Measuring jug and spoons
Wooden spoons for mixing
Large metal spoon for folding in ingredients
Sieve
Wooden skewer

Conversion Tables

WEIGHT

25g - 1oz

50g - 1¾oz

75g - 2¾oz

100g - 3½oz

150g - 5½oz

175g - 6oz

200g - 7oz

225g - 8oz

250g - 9oz

275g - 9¾oz

300g - 10½oz

350g - 12oz

375g - 13oz

400g - 14oz

425g - 15oz

450g - 1lb

500g - 1lb 2oz

VOLUME

1.25ml - ¼tsp

2.5ml - ½tsp

15ml - 1tsp

30ml - 1fl oz

50ml - 2fl oz

100ml - 3½fl oz

150ml - 5fl oz - ¼ pint

200ml - 7fl oz

300ml - 10 fl oz - ½ pint

500ml - 18fl oz

600ml - 20fl oz - 1 pint

700ml - 1¼ pints

850ml - 1½ pints

1L - 1¾ pints

1.2L - 2 pints

Amaretti Crunch Cake

Ingredients

Cake Ingredients

265g (1¼ cup) soft butter
200g (1 cup) caster sugar
210g (1¾ cup) self raising flour
4 large eggs
85g (¾ cup) ground almonds

Filling and topping

170g (1¾ cup) amaretti biscuits, roughly broken or mini size

Method

1. Preheat the oven to 170°C / 325°F / gas 3
2. Line a 7x11ins (18x28cm) traybake tin with parchment paper
3. Place all the cake ingredients into a bowl and beat using an electric hand whisk until well blended
4. Spread half the cake mixture in the tin
5. Scatter over half of the amaretti biscuits
6. Cover with the remaining cake mixture and spread evenly.
7. Scatter the remaining amaretti pressing in slightly
8. Bake for 50 minutes until a skewer inserted into the middle comes out clean
9. Allow to cool in the tin and turn out on a serving plate.

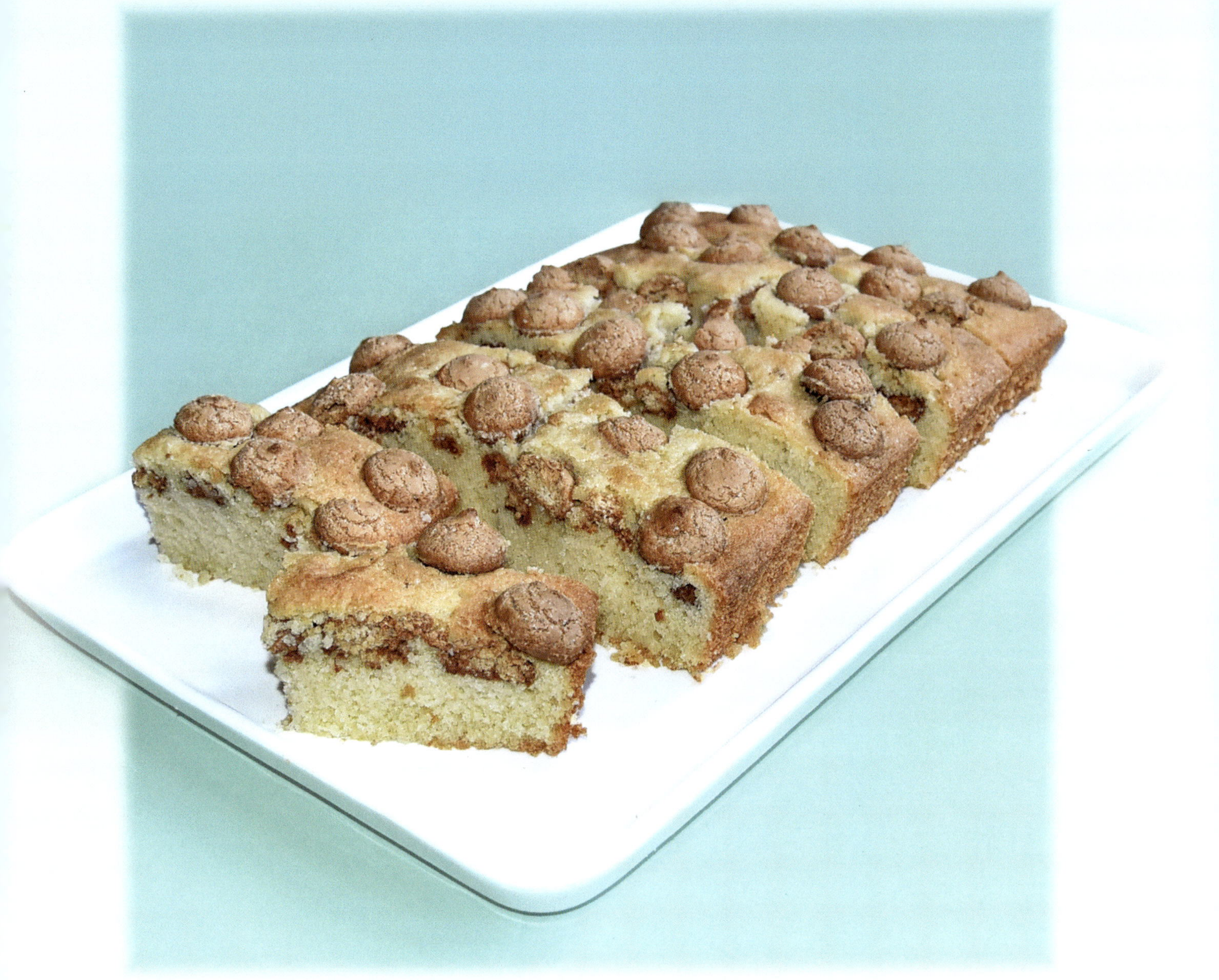

Apricot and Marzipan Cake

Ingredients

Base
120g (½ cup) unsalted butter, softened
275g (1½ cup) caster sugar
3 eggs
1 teaspoon vanilla extract
1 teaspoon almond extract
170g (1¼ cup) plain flour
25g (¼ cup) self raising flour
¼ teaspoon salt
¼ teaspoon bicarbonate of soda
80g (¾ cup) ground almonds
125ml soured cream

75g (½ cup) marzipan/almond paste, chopped into small chunks
130g (1 cup) soft dried apricots, chopped

Topping
220g (¾ cup) greek set yogurt
130g (¾ cup) apricot jam
60g (¾ cup) toasted almond flakes
1 tablespoon icing sugar

Method

Base
1. Preheat the oven to 170°C / 325°F / gas 3
2. Line a 7x11ins (18x28cm) traybake tin with parchment paper.
3. Cream the butter and sugar using an electric hand whisk until fluffy,
4. Add the eggs gradually, beating well.
5. Beat in the vanilla and almond extract.
6. Whisk in the flours, salt, bicarb of soda and almonds into the batter gradually, alternating with spoonfuls of sour cream.
7. Fold in the apricots and the marzipan
8. Spoon into the tin
9. Bake for 30 minutes then reduce the oven to 150°C/ 300°F/ gas 2 and continue baking for another 30 minutes
A skewer inserted into the middle should come out clean, but don't overcook.
10. Leave to cool for 15 minutes and turn it onto a wire rack. Leave to cool.

Topping
For the topping, mix the yogurt and jam to create a marbled effect. Spoon on top of the cake and scatter with the almonds.
Dust with icing sugar
Store covered in the fridge

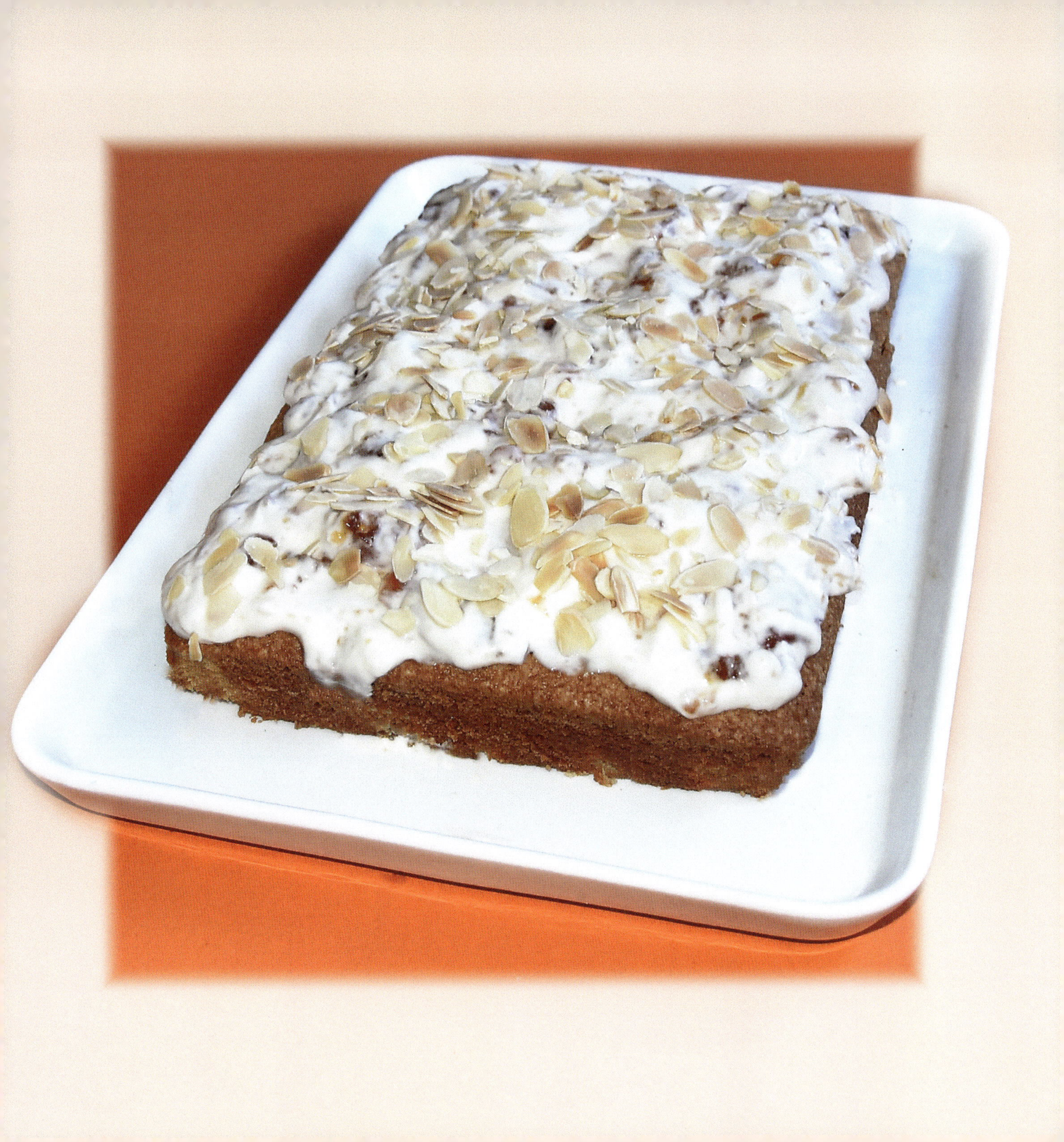

Baked Cheesecake

Ingredients

Base
200g (2 cups) digestive biscuits/graham crackers
70g (¼ cup) unsalted butter, melted

Cheesecake
450g (2 cups) full fat soft/cream cheese
125g (¾ cup) caster sugar
3 eggs, separated
25g (¾ cup) cornflour/fine cornmeal
1 teaspoon vanilla essence
142ml soured cream

Method

Base
1. Preheat the oven to 150°C / 300°F / gas 2
2. Line a 7 x 11ins (18 x 28cm) traybake tin with parchment paper
3. Put the biscuits in a plastic bag and crush with a rolling pin.
4. Combine the biscuit crumbs with the melted butter and press into the base of the traybake tin.

Cheesecake
1. Place the rest of the ingredients except for the egg whites in a bowl and combine using a hand whisk.
2. Whisk the egg whites in a separate bowl until stiff and fold into the cheese mixture.
3. Pour onto the biscuit base. The cheesecake will not rise so the tin can be filled to the top
4. Bake for 1½ hours
5. Turn off the oven and leave in the oven until cold.
6. When cold place in the fridge for a couple of hours before removing from the tin and serving.

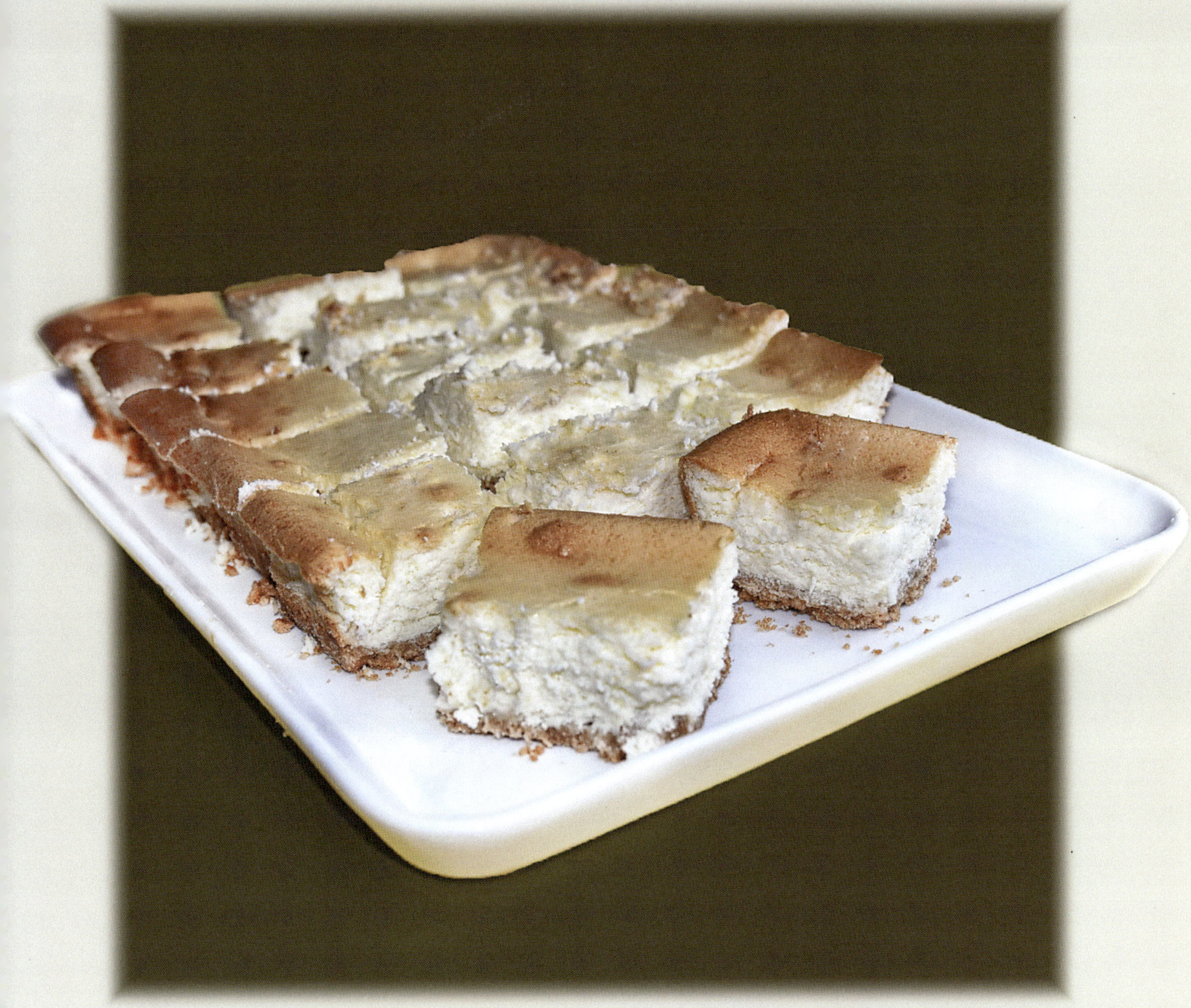

Banana and Pineapple Cake

Ingredients

300g (2½ cup) self-raising flour
½ teaspoon baking powder
200g (1 cup) caster sugar
1 teaspoon ground cinnamon
2 cardamom pods, cracked open and seeds crushed
2½ teaspoons ground nutmeg

2 ripe bananas, thinly sliced
225ml vegetable oil
3 eggs

250g (1 cup) pineapple chunks, drained from a can or fresh
80g (¾ cup) walnuts

Topping
200g (1 cup) full-fat soft/cream cheese
150g (¾ cup) softened unsalted block butter
100g (¾ cup) sifted icing sugar

Dessicated coconut for sprinkling (optional)

Method

1. Preheat the oven to 180°C / 350°F / gas 4
2. Line a 7 x 11ins (18 x 28cm) traybake tin with parchment paper
3. Place all the dry ingredients in a large bowl
4. In a separate bowl whisk the bananas through the oil and eggs until broken up and well combined
5. Make a well in the centre of the dry ingredients and fold in the wet mixture until combined.
6. Mix through the pineapple and walnuts
7. Spoon the mixture into the tin and even out the top
8. Bake in the centre of the oven for 40 minutes or until a skewer inserted into the middle comes out clean
9. Leave to cool completely in the tin before removing.

Topping
Place all the topping ingredients into a bowl and briefly beat till combined. Do not overbeat or the mixture will become too soft and runny.
Chill in the fridge for 30 minutes before spreading over the cake and sprinkling with dessicated coconut (if using)

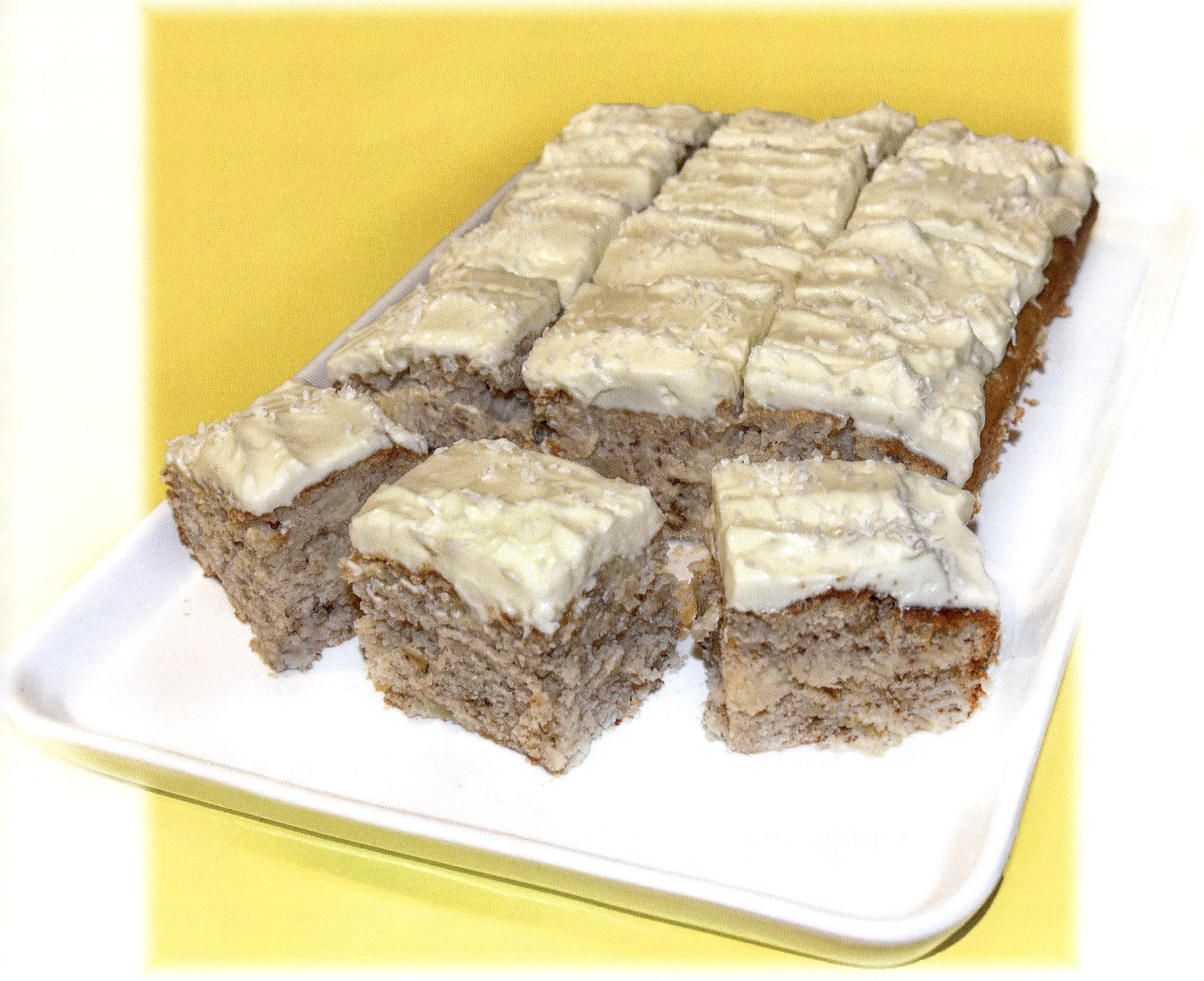

Berry and Coconut Slices

Ingredients

Fruit Layer

400g (2 cups) blueberries (fresh or frozen)
400g (2 cups) blackberries or raspberries (fresh or frozen)
80g (½ cup) caster sugar
50ml water

Shortbread layer

115g (¾ cup) caster sugar
250g (1 cup) butter
275g (2¼ cup) plain flour
80g (1 cup) dessicated coconut

Sponge Topping

2 eggs
75g (½ cup) caster sugar
60g (½ cup) self raising flour
2 limes, zest and juice

Method

1. Preheat the oven to 200°C / 400°F / gas 6.
2. Line a 7 x 11ins (18 x 28cm) traybake tin with parchment paper

To make Fruit layer

1. Place all the fruit layer ingredients in a large pan
2. Bring to the boil, cover and simmer for 10 minutes.
3. Remove the lid and continue to simmer for 30 minutes, stirring frequently, until sticky. Allow to cool completely, then put in the fridge for a couple of hours. The fruit will set to a jam like consistency.

To make the Shortbread

1. Put all the ingredients in a bowl and combine with an electric beater or a food processor.
2. Press into the prepared tin and bake for 20-25 minutes until golden. Leave to cool completely.
3. Spread the berry mixture over the shortbread.

To make the sponge topping

1. Reduce the oven to 170°C / 325°F / gas 3
2. Beat the eggs with the sugar until thick and pale. Stir in the self raising flour, lime zest and juice.
3. Top the traybake with the lime sponge and bake for 45-50 minutes until the sponge has set.
4. Allow to cool, keep in the fridge, then cut into slices.

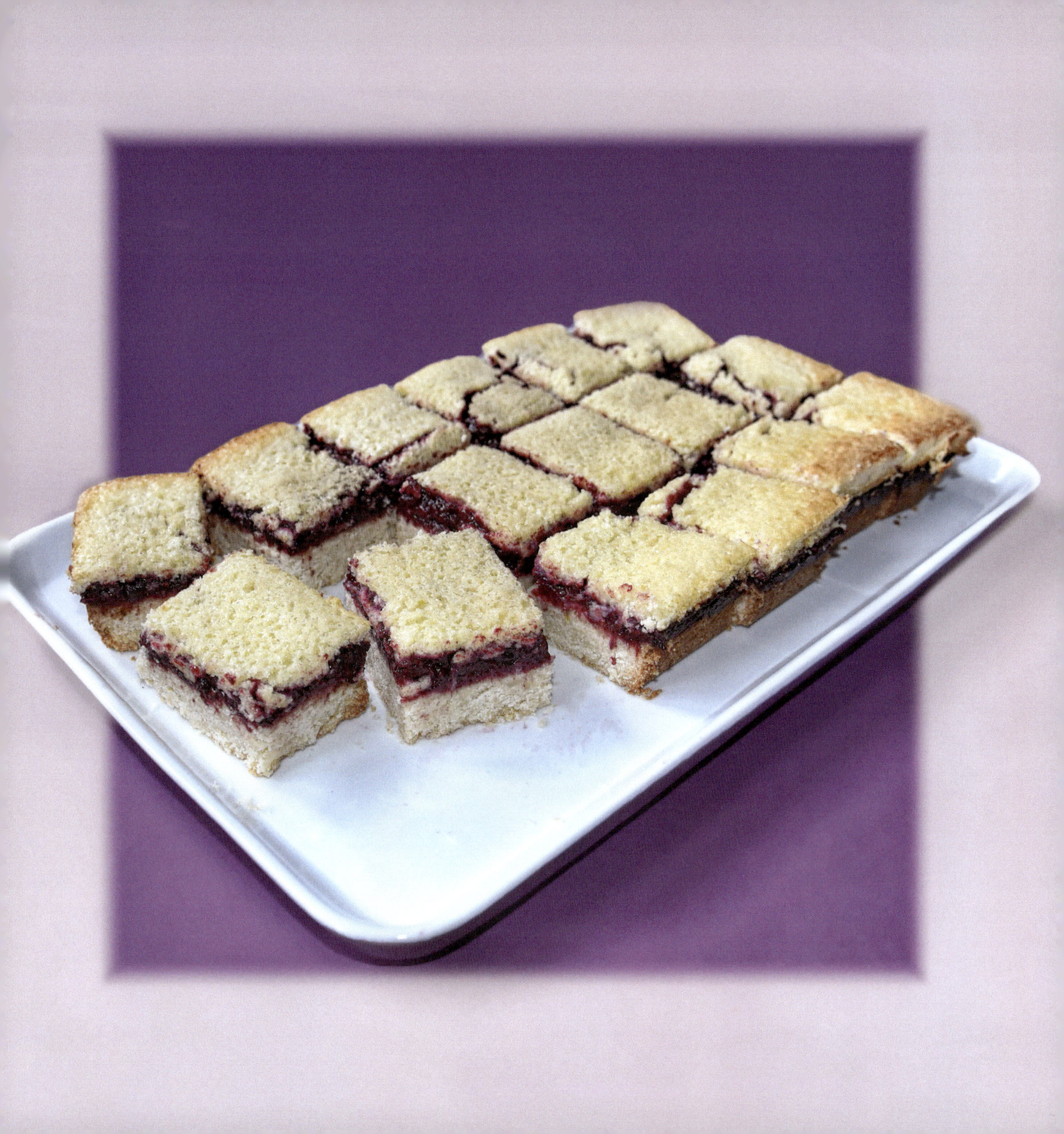

Caramel and Pear Cake

Ingredients

125g (½ cup) unsalted butter
395g (1 1/3 cups) Carnation caramel or any caramel spread
2 medium eggs
1 teaspoon caramel flavouring (optional)
225g (1¾ cup) self raising flour
2 teaspoons baking powder
2 teaspoons ground cinnamon
300g (2 cups) ripe Conference pears, peeled cored and diced
2 tablespoons milk

Method

1. Preheat oven to 170°C / 325°F / gas 3
2. Line a 7 x 11ins (18 x 28cm) traybake tin with parchment paper
3. In a large bowl beat the butter and 225g of the caramel (reserve the rest) together with an electric hand whisk until well combined
4. Beat in the eggs one at a time and add the caramel flavoring if using
5. Sift over the flour, baking powder and cinnamon and fold together with a metal spoon
6. Stir in the pears and milk
7. Spoon the cake mix into the prepared tin and smooth the top
8. Bake for 45 minutes until golden on top and a skewer inserted in the middle comes out clean
9. Allow the cake to cool in the tin then remove on to a serving plate.

Topping

Warm the rest of the caramel in a saucepan or microwave until pourable.
Drizzle over the top of the cake and serve

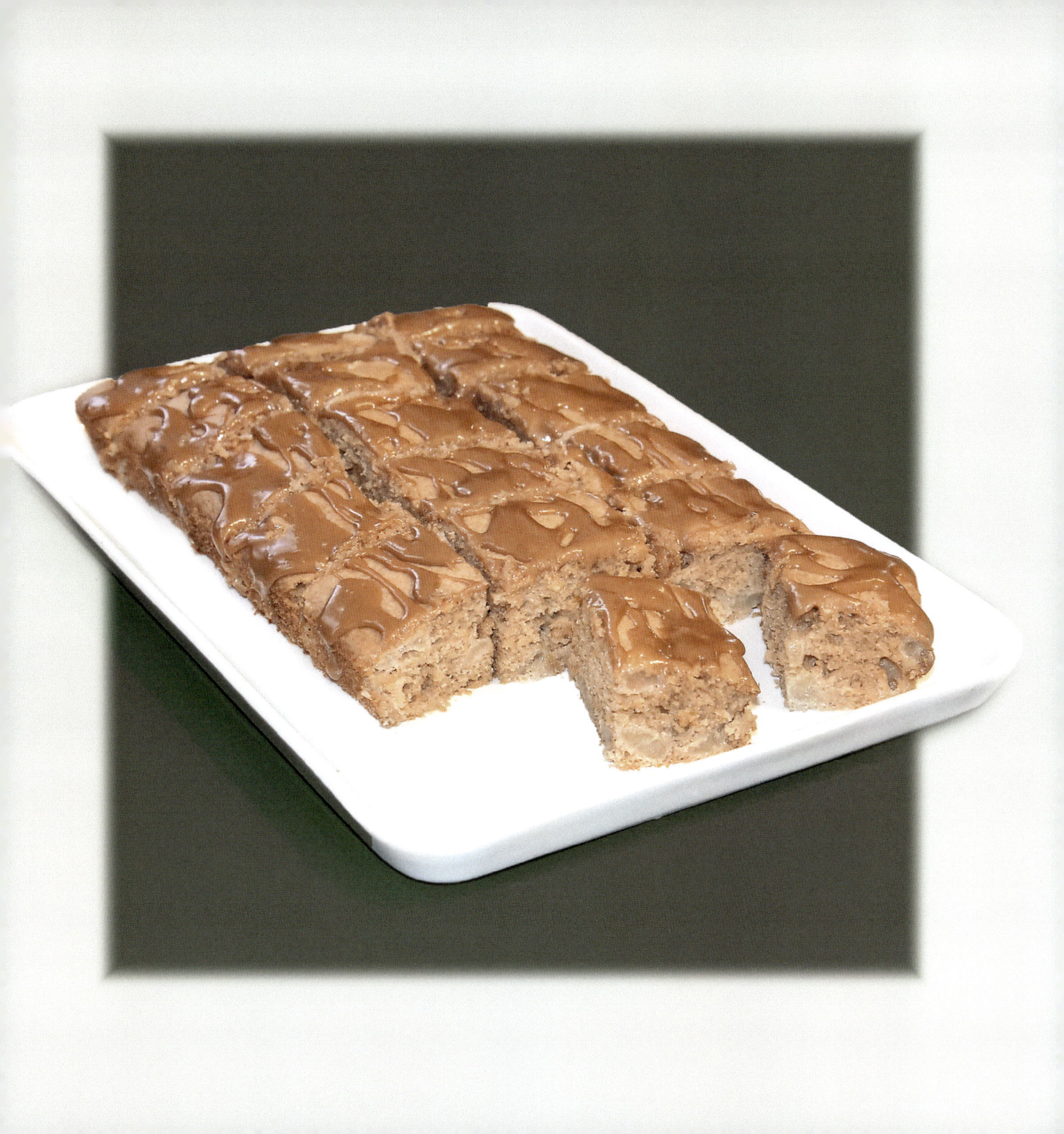

Choc Chip Slices

Ingredients

4 large eggs
150g (¾ cup) light brown sugar
250g (1 cup) salted butter, melted
1 tablespoon) vanilla extract
200g (1¾ cup) self-raising flour
150g (1 cup) dark chocolate, roughly chopped
150g (1 cup) milk chocolate, roughly chopped

Method

1. Preheat oven to 180°C / 350°F / gas 4
2. Line a 7 x 11ins (18 x 28cm) traybake tin with parchment paper
3. Whisk the eggs with the sugar until pale
4. Beat in the melted butter and vanilla
5. Sift the flour on to the mixture and gradually fold in
6. Mix in the chocolate chunks
7. Spread the mixture evenly in the tin and bake for 25 minutes until just cooked.
8. Leave to cool overnight then cut into bars.

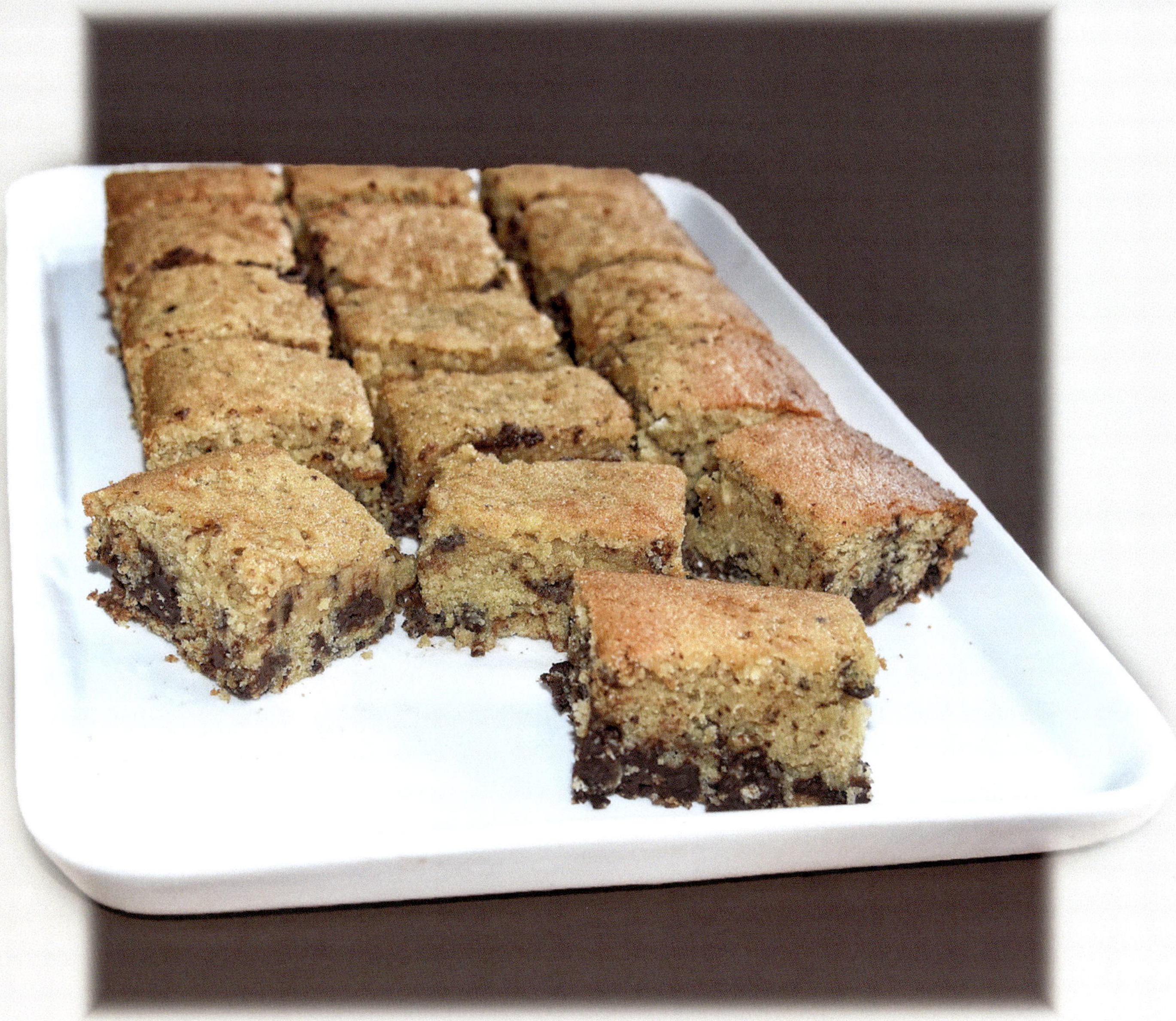

Chocolate Meringue Traybake

Ingredients

240g (1½ cup) dark chocolate
180g (¾ cup) unsalted butter
2 eggs
4 egg yolks (keep the whites for the meringue below)
90g (½ cup) light brown sugar
1 teaspoon vanilla extract
50g (½ cup) plain flour, sifted
½ teaspoon baking powder, sifted
50g (½ cup) ground almonds

Meringue

4 egg whites
220g (1 cup) caster sugar
1 teaspoon white vinegar
3 teaspoons cornflour
25g (¼ cup) cocoa powder

Method

1. Preheat oven to 170°C / 325°F / gas 3
2. Line a 7 x 11ins (18 x 28cm) traybake tin with parchment paper
3. Place the chocolate and butter in a saucepan over a low heat and stir until melted. Allow to cool slightly.
4. Place the 2 eggs, extra 4 yolks, brown sugar and vanilla in a bowl and whisk for 3–4 minutes or until pale and thick.
5. Add the chocolate mixture, the flour, baking powder and almonds and gently fold to combine.
6. Pour into the tin and bake for 35–40 minutes. Allow to cool in the tin slightly.

Meringue

1. Increase the oven temperature to 180°C, 350°F, Gas mark 4
2. Place the egg whites in a clean bowl and whisk until soft peaks form.
3. Add the sugar, 1 tablespoon at a time, whisking for 30 seconds before adding more.
4. Add the vinegar and whisk for 2–3 minutes or until the meringue is thick and glossy.
5. Add the cornflour and cocoa and fold to combine.
5. Spoon the meringue mixture onto the cake and spread evenly. Return the cake to the oven for 20–25 minutes or until the meringue is golden and crisp. Allow to cool in the tin.

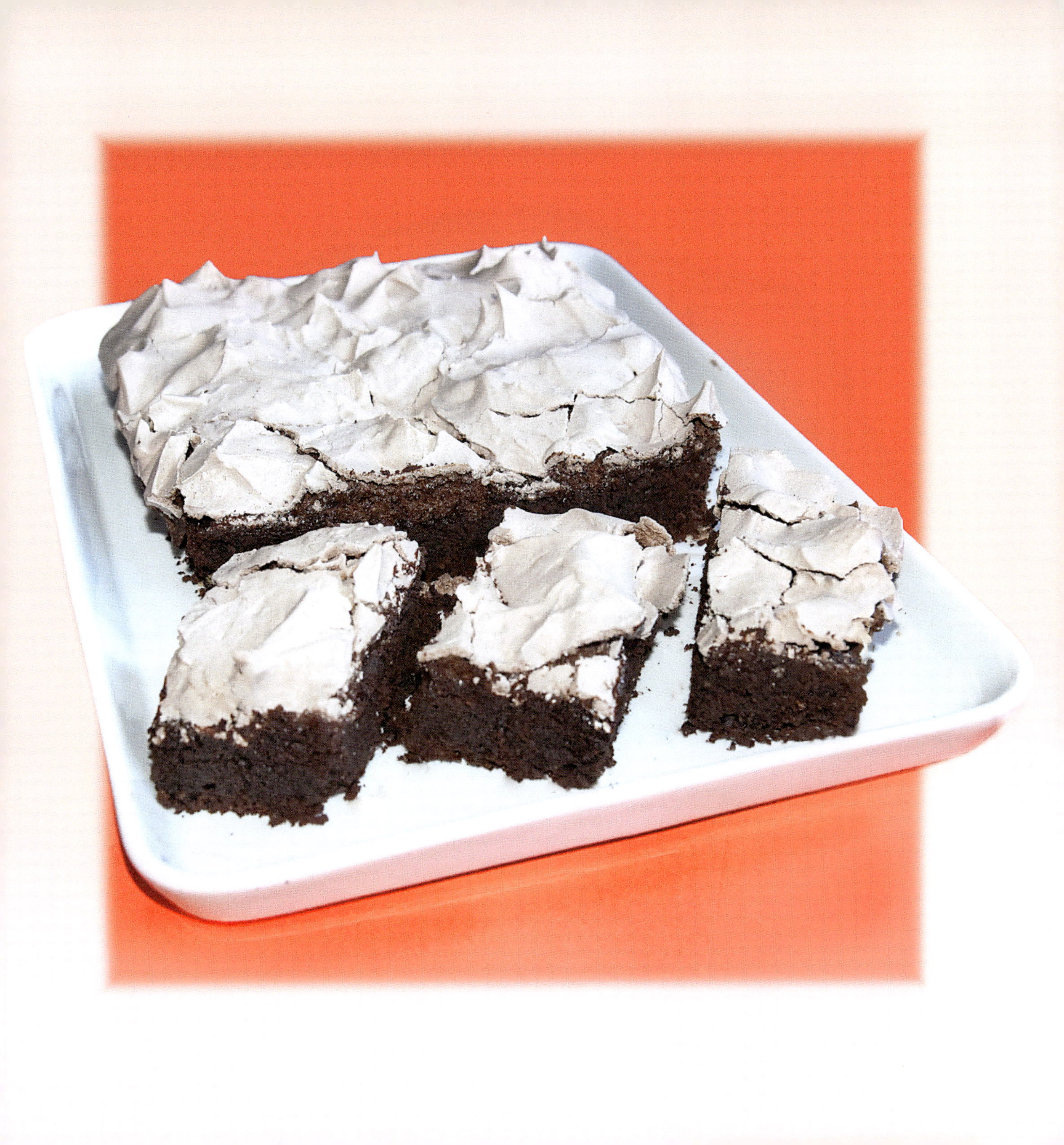

Coconut Chocolate Slices

Ingredients

300g (2 cups) dark chocolate
100g (½ cup) butter
150g (¾ cup) caster sugar
2 medium eggs, lightly beaten
200g (2¼ cup) desiccated coconut
200g (1¼ cup) glace cherries, cut in half

Method

1. Line a 7 x 11ins (18 x 28cm) traybake tin with parchment paper
2. Melt the chocolate in a bowl placed over a pan of simmering water
3. Pour the chocolate into the prepared tin spreading it out to cover the base evenly.
4. Put aside to set.
5. When chocolate is set, preheat the oven to 140°C / 275°F / gas 1
6. Cream the butter and sugar together until light.
7. Beat in the eggs and coconut.
8. Fold in the cherries.
9. Spread the coconut mixture over the chocolate base in an even layer
10. Bake for 1 hour until golden
11. Leave to cool in the tin then chill so that the chocolate sets
12. Take out of the tin and cut into pieces

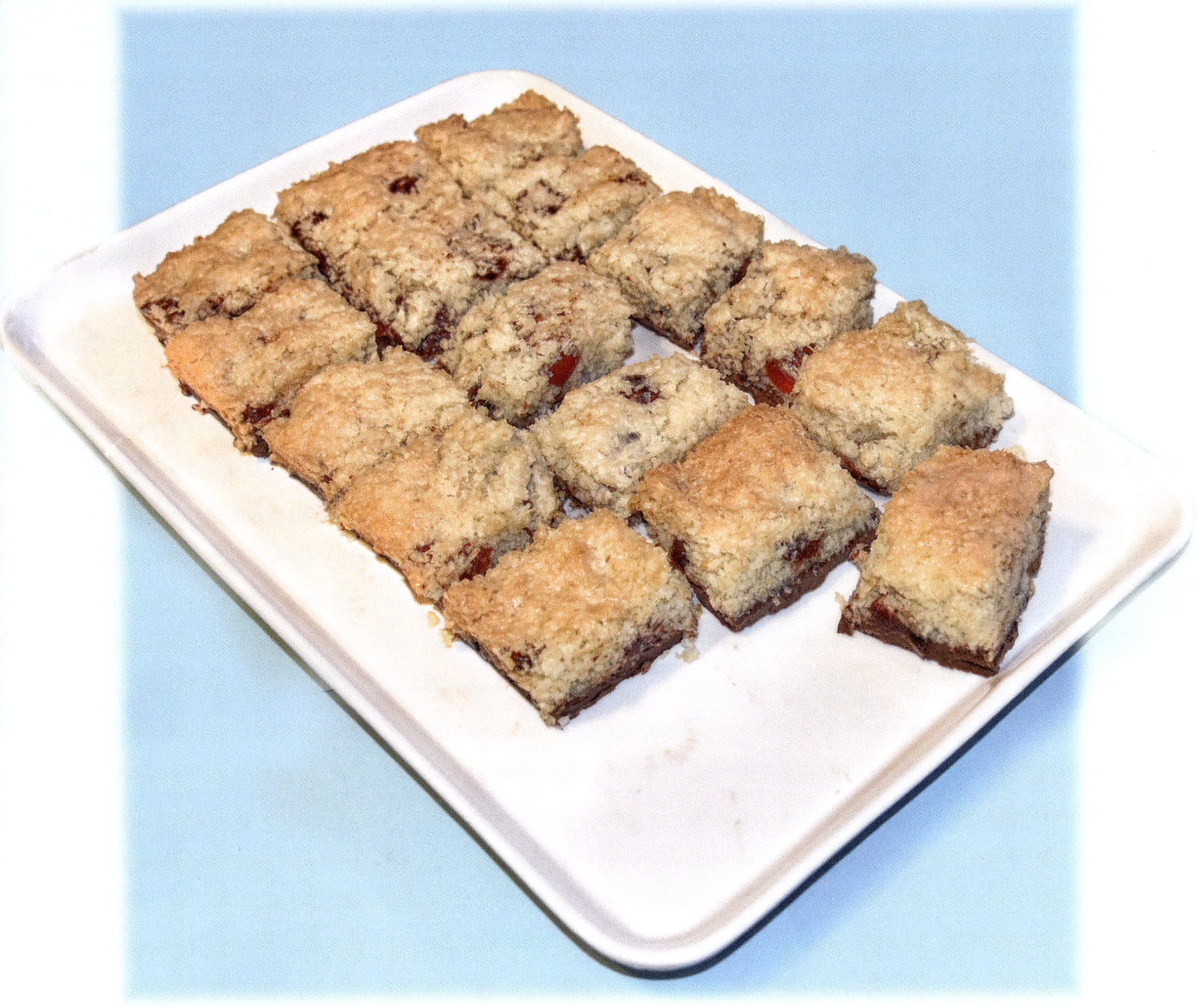

Double Chocolate & Nut Brownie

Ingredients

300g (2 cups) dark chocolate,
100g (½ cup) unsalted butter
4 medium eggs
225g (1 cup) soft brown sugar
2 teaspoons vanilla extract
120g (1 cup) plain flour
¼ teaspoon baking powder
100g (1 cup) pecans or walnuts, roughly chopped
pinch of salt

Method

1. Preheat the oven to 180°C / gas 4 / 350°F
2. Line a 7 x 11ins (18 x 28cm) traybake tin with parchment paper
3. Melt 200g (1¼ cup) of the chocolate in a bowl set over a pan of simmering water.
4. Add the butter and stir until melted, leave to cool.
5. Chop the remaining chocolate into chunks and reserve.
6. Beat the eggs sugar and vanilla until pale and creamy.
7. Fold in the flour, baking powder, nuts, chopped chocolate and salt.
8. Stir in the cooled melted chocolate.
9. Pour into the tin
10. Bake for 25 minutes until set.
11. Leave to cool in the tin before cutting into squares.

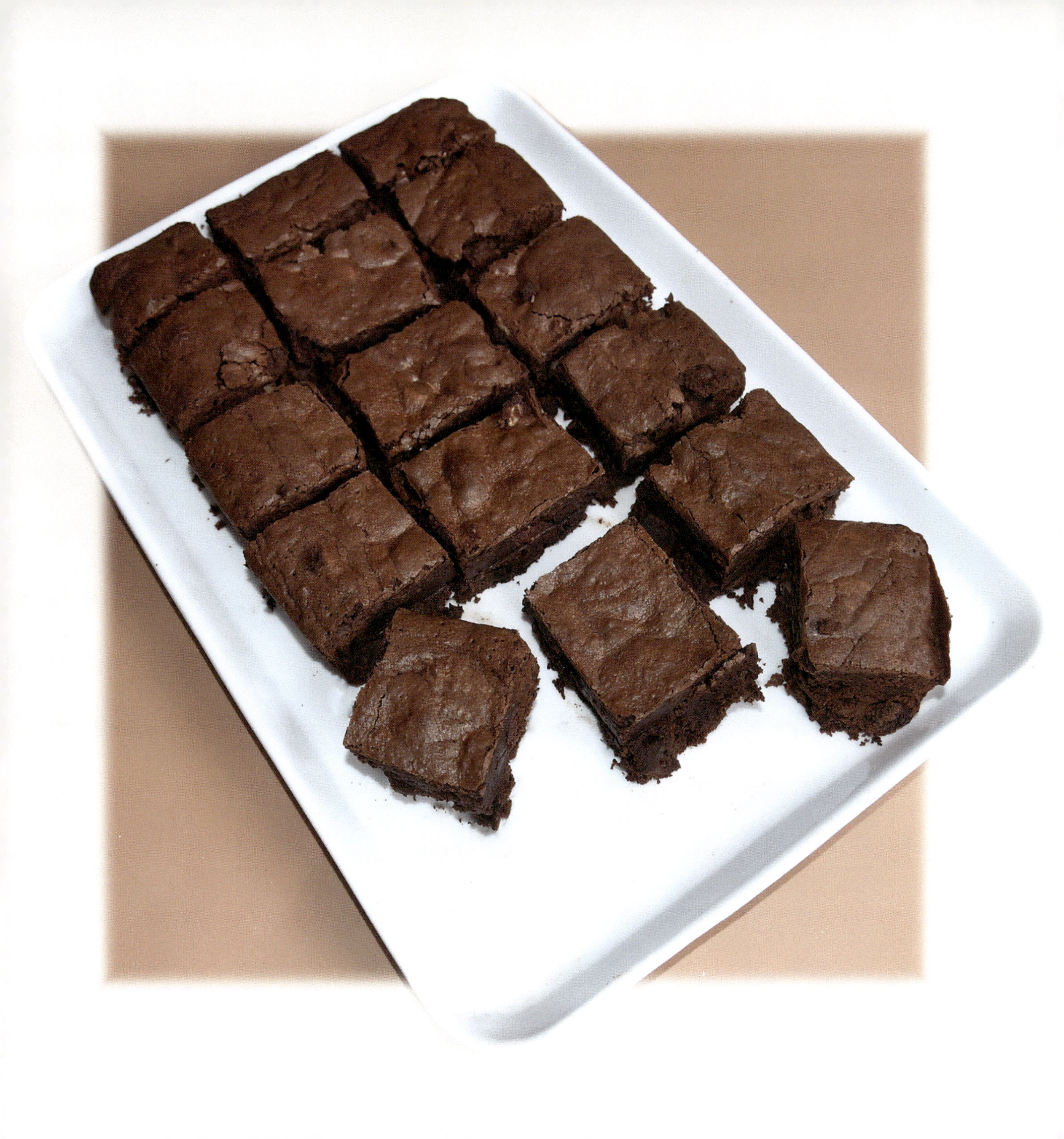

Easter Slices

Ingredients

Base

300g (2 cups) plain flour
150g (¾ cup) butter
90g (½ cup) sugar
1 large egg
2-3 tablespoons milk

Filling

160g (½ cup) morello cherry jam or marmalade

Topping

240g (1½ cup) plain dark chocolate/chips
95g (½ cup) double cream
2 tablespoons butter
1 tablespoon honey

Decoration (optional)

Almonds
Cherries
Sweets
Dried fruit
Piped icing patterns

Method

1. Preheat the oven to 180°C / gas 4 / 350°F
2. Line a 7 x 11ins (18 x 28cm) traybake tin with parchment paper
3. Rub the butter into the flour until the mixture resembles breadcrumbs
4. Add the sugar, egg and milk and knead into a dough
5. Press the dough into the tin
6. Bake for 30 minutes until the dough begins to turn golden.
7. Leave to cool in the oven

Filling

Warm the jam and spread over the base. If the jam has large pieces of fruit, blitz with a hand blender or press through a sieve.

Topping

1. Heat the cream until just beginning to bubble
2. Add the chocolate, butter and honey and stir until chocolate has melted
3. Pour the chocolate over the jam layer

4. Decorate

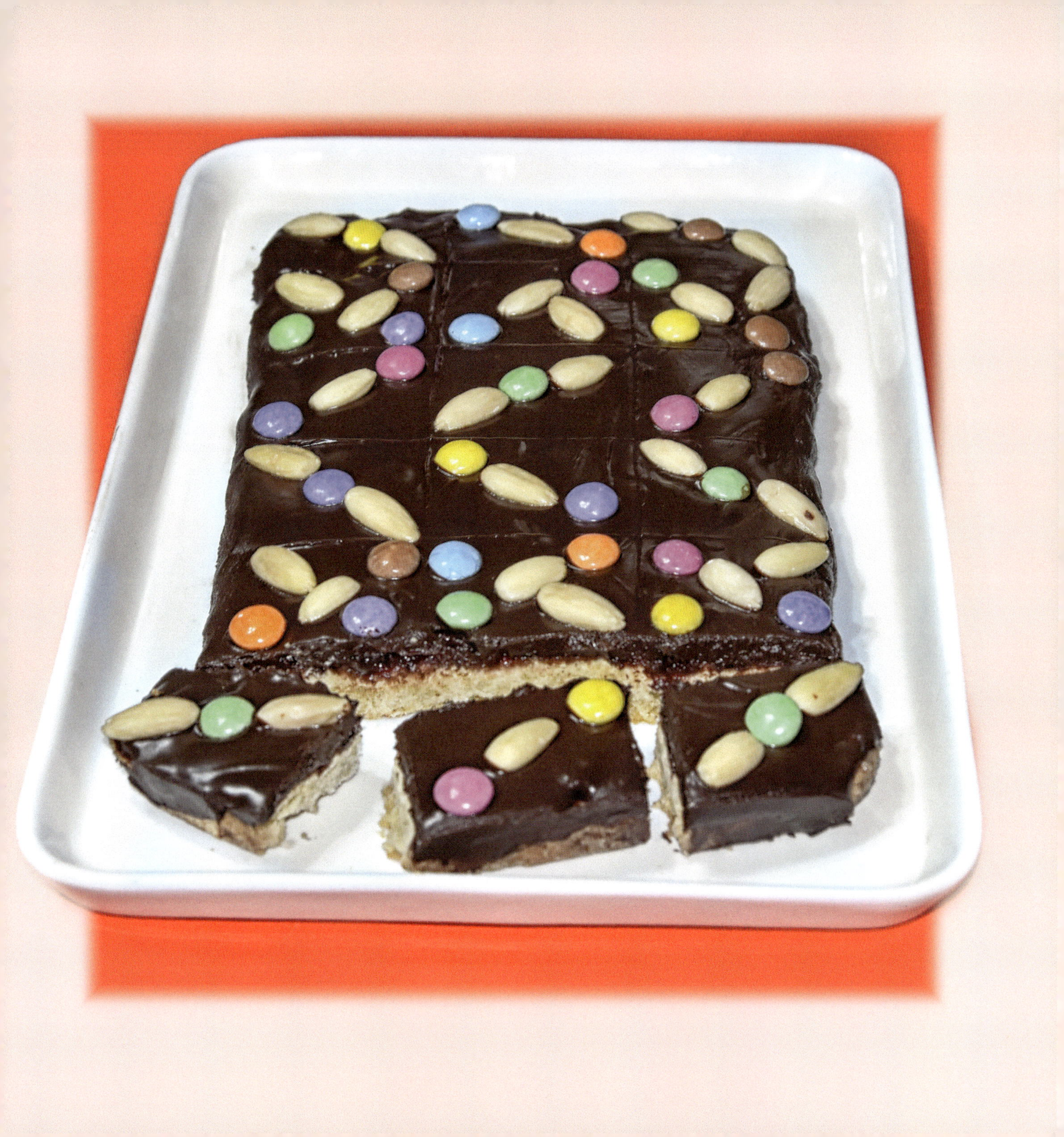

Fruit Crumble Sponge

Ingredients

Fruit Layer
675g (5 cups) prepared fruit - or approximately 12 Plums or apricots, stoned and cut in halves or quarters.
Apples or pears peeled and sliced.
Soft fruits such as raspberries, blackcurrants, gooseberries etc

Cake Layer
125g (½ cup) butter
125g (¾ cup) caster sugar
2 eggs
1 teaspoon vanilla essence
175g (1½ cup) plain flour
1 teaspoon baking powder
50g (¼ cup) cornflour
50g (½ cup) ground almonds

Topping
125g (½ cup) butter
50g (¼ cup) caster sugar
50g (½ cup) ground almonds
50g (¼ cup) cornflour
50g (½ cup) plain flour

Method

1. Preheat the oven to 180°C / gas 4 / 350°F
2. Line a 7 x 11ins (18 x 28cm) traybake tin with parchment paper

Cake Layer
1. Cream butter and sugar together until pale
2. Beat in the eggs and vanilla
3. Fold in the flour, baking powder, cornflour and almonds.
4. Spread the mixture in the prepared tin
5. Cover with the prepared fruit

Topping
1. In a separate bowl rub together all the topping ingredients to form large crumbs
2. Sprinkle over the fruit
3. Bake for 1 to 1¼ hours.
4. Allow to cool in the tin before cutting into slices and serving.

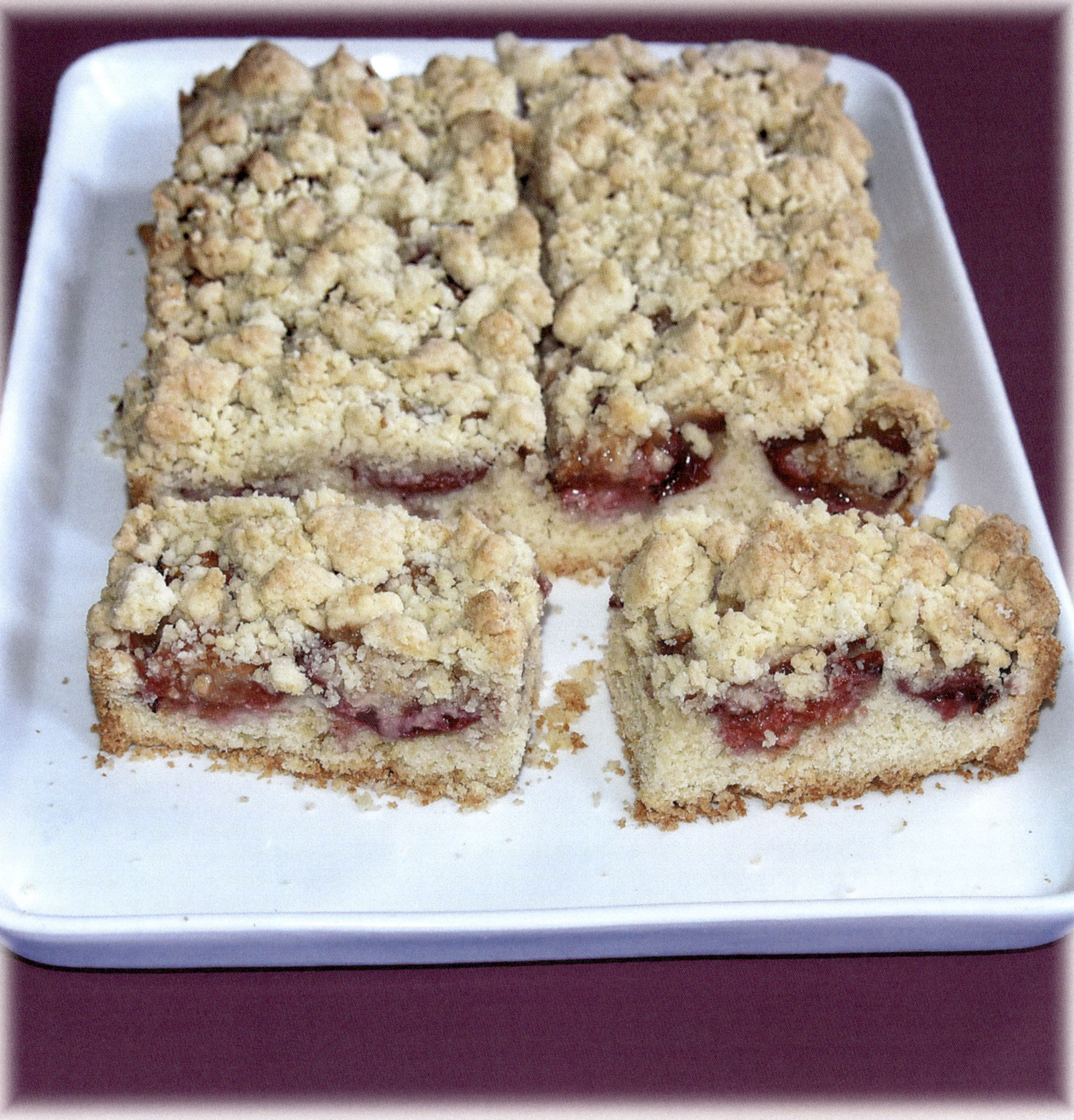

Fruit Curd Bars

Ingredients

170g (¾ cup) salted butter
285g (2¼ cup) plain flour
50g (¼ cup) caster sugar
½ teaspoon baking powder
1 egg yolk

Curd Layer
320g (1 cup) of any fruit curd, lemon, orange, passionfruit, etc

Crumb Topping
30g (¼ cup) demerara sugar
50g (¼ cup) jumbo oats
30g (½ cup) flaked almonds
30g (½ cup) pecans, chopped

Method

1. Preheat the oven to 190°C / 375°F / gas 5
2. Line a 7 x 11ins (18 x 28cm) traybake tin with parchment paper
3. Using your fingertips, rub the butter into the flour.
4. Stir in the caster sugar then remove 1/3 of the mixture (about 175g) and set aside in a bowl.
5. Add the baking powder and egg yolk to the remaining mixture and mix to form a dough.
6. Tip into the baking tin and press down to form an even layer.
7. Bake for 15 minutes, then allow to cool for 10 minutes.

Curd Layer
Spread the fruit curd over the biscuit base.

Crumb Topping
1. Add the demerara sugar, oats and nuts to the reserved mixture, with ½ tbsp water.
2. Mix everything together with a large spoon to form a crumble mixture
3. Sprinkle over the cake.
4. Bake for 20-25 minutes, or until lightly golden. Remove and allow to cool completely in the tin.
5. Remove from the tin and slice into bars.

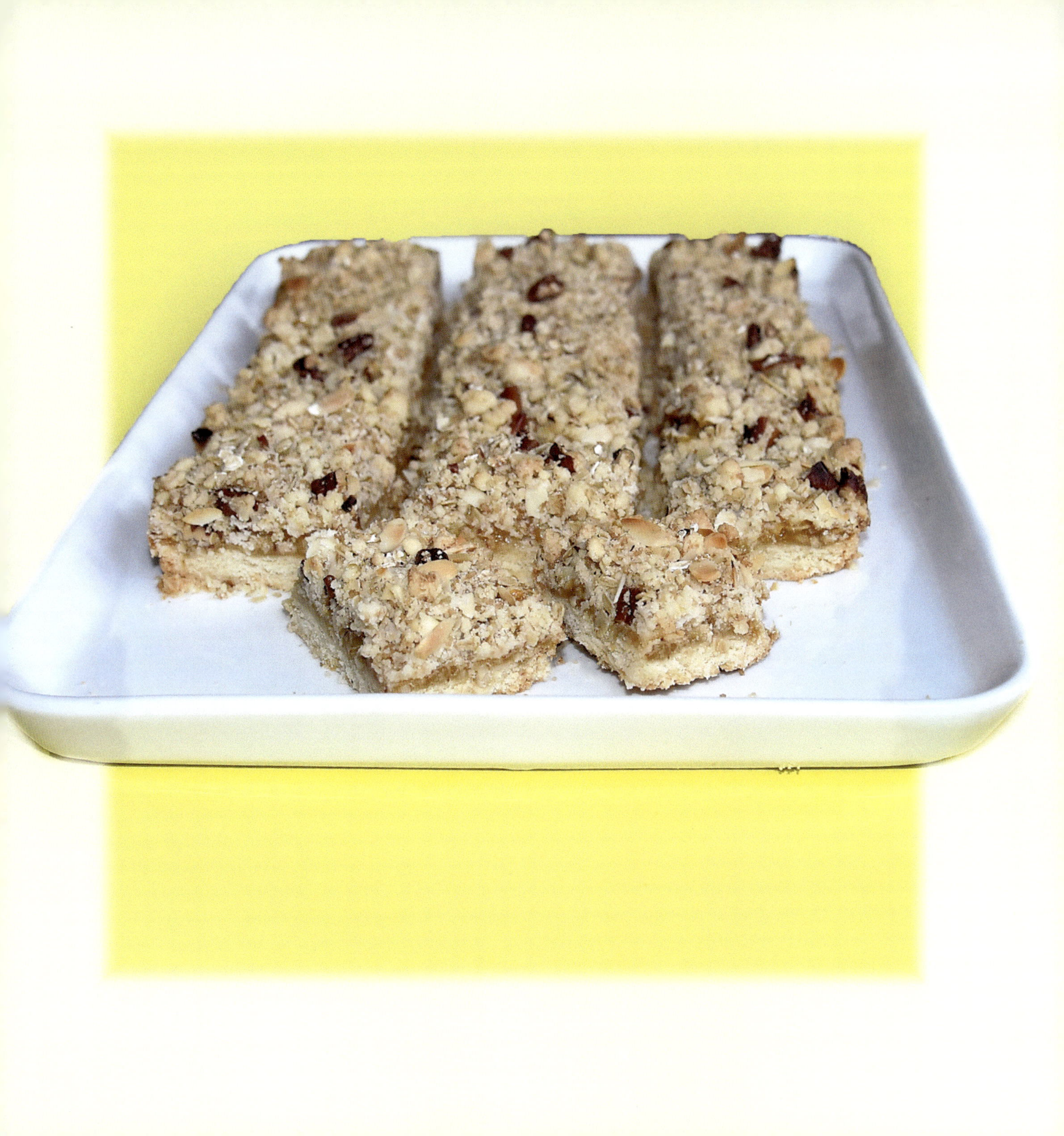

Fudgy Coffee and Nut Shortbread

Ingredients

Shortbread layer
150g (¾ cup) salted butter
75g (1/3 cup) light brown muscovado sugar
225g (1¾ cup) plain flour
2 tablespoons maple syrup

Coffee topping
150g (1½ cup) walnuts or pecans
75g (¼ cup) unsalted butter
190g (1 cup) light brown muscovado sugar
2 tablespoons instant coffee
7 tablespoons maple syrup
2 tablespoons plain flour
3 eggs

Decoration
50g (¼ cup) dark chocolate
1 teaspoon vegetable oil

Method

1. Preheat the oven to 180°C / gas 4 / 350°F
2. Line a 7 x 11ins (18 x 28cm) traybake tin with parchment paper

Shortbread layer
1. Beat the butter and sugar until pale.
2. Fold in the flour and maple syrup.
3. Press into the tin, smooth the surface and prick with a fork
4. Freeze for 10 minutes
5. Bake the shortbread for 20 minutes until golden

Coffee topping
1. Toast the walnuts in the oven for 8 minutes and roughly chop
2. Melt the butter in a pan and simmer for 3 minutes.
3. Take the pan off the heat then whisk in the remaining topping ingredients and stir in the toasted nuts.
4. Pour onto the shortbread and bake for 40 minutes until set.
5. Cool completely in the tin

Decoration
Melt the chocolate and oil in a bowl set over a pan of simmering water. Drizzle over the traybake and allow to set before cutting into squares.

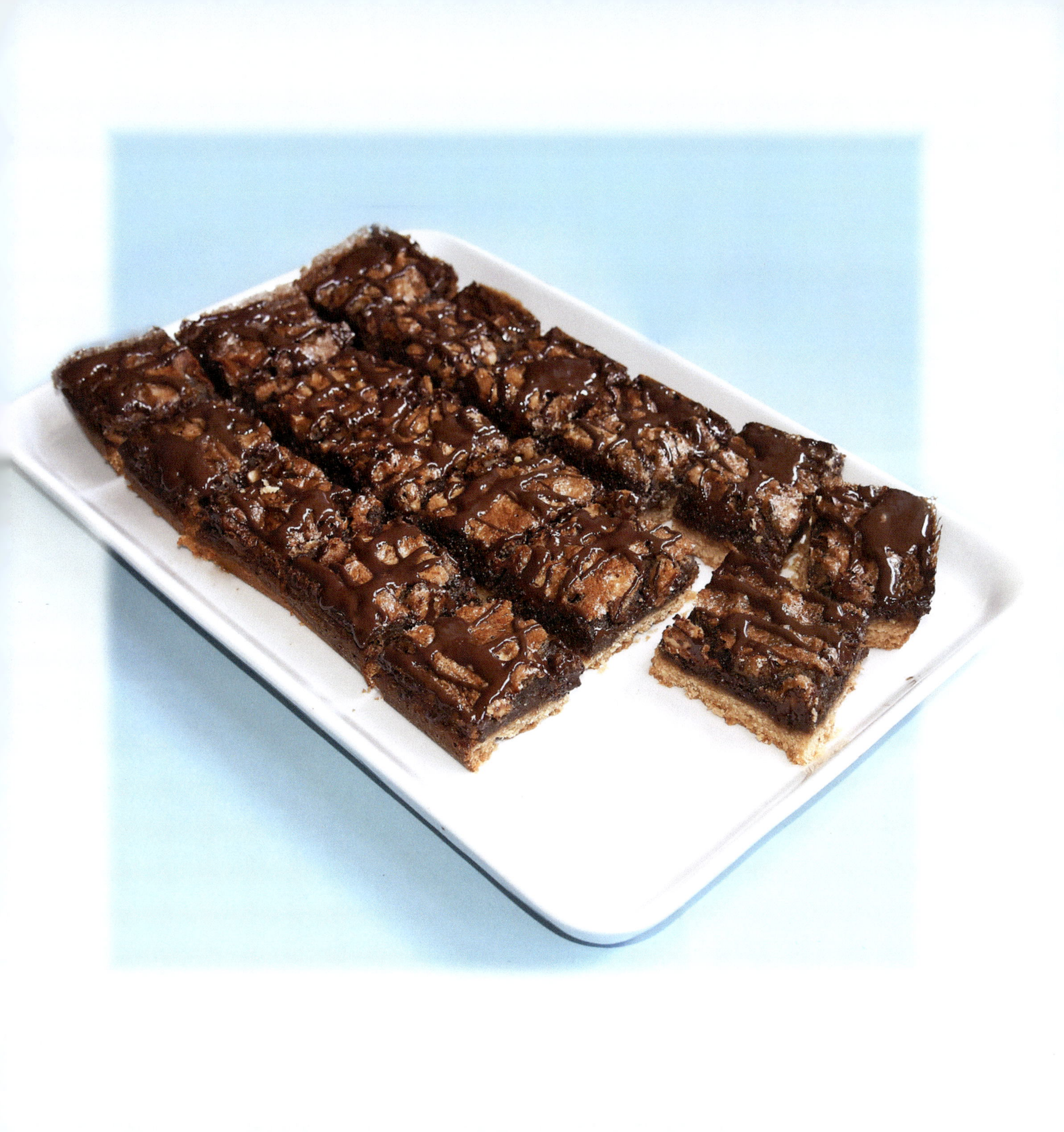

Ginger Flapjack Bars

Ingredients

220g (1 cup) butter
110g (½ cup) demerara sugar
110g (¼ cup) golden syrup

2½ teaspoons ground ginger
Pinch of salt
115g (½ cup) chopped stem ginger
375g (2½ cup) rolled oats

Method

1. Preheat the oven to 150°C / gas 2 / 300°F
2. Line a 7 x 11ins (18 x 28cm) traybake tin with parchment paper
3. Melt the butter, sugar and golden syrup in a large pan
4. Remove from the heat and mix in the rest of the ingredients
5. Press the mixture firmly into the tin with the back of a spoon
6. Bake for 40 minutes
7. Remove the tin from the oven and allow to cool before cutting into slices.

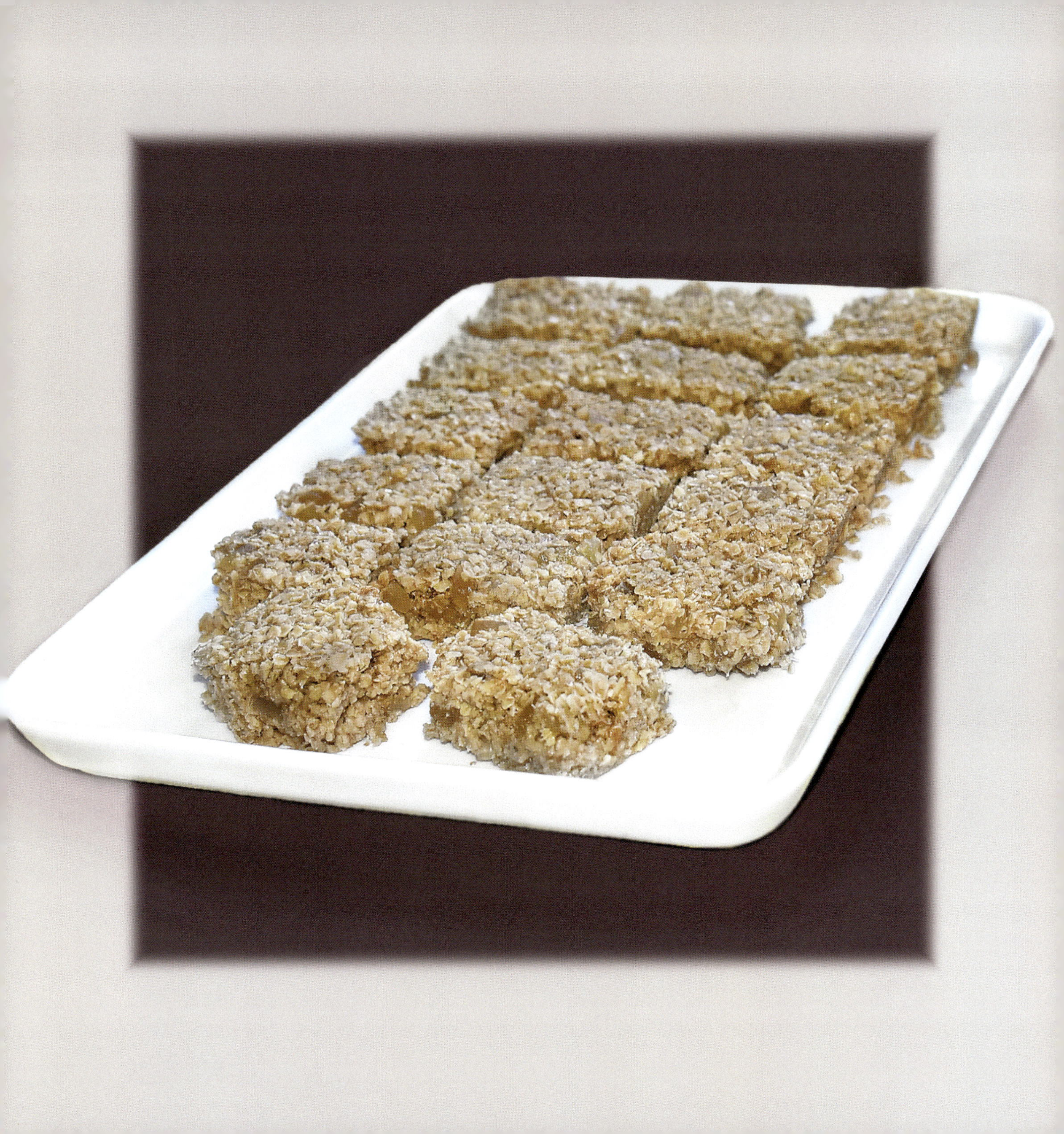

Lemon, Honey & Polenta cake

Ingredients

225g (1 cup) unsalted butter
225g (¾ cup) runny honey
5 medium eggs, separated
2 lemons, zest
300g (2¾ cup) ground almonds
150g (1 cup) polenta
2 teaspoons baking powder
½ teaspoon fine salt

Honey syrup

100g (¼ cup) runny honey
1 lemon, juice

Method

1. Preheat the oven to 170°C / 325°F / gas 3
2. Line a 7 x 11ins (18 x 28cm) traybake tin with parchment paper
3. In a large bowl, use electric beaters to cream the butter and honey together, until light and fluffy.
4. Beat in the egg yolks and lemon zest, then the almonds, polenta, baking powder and salt.
5. In a separate bowl, with clean beaters, whisk the egg whites to stiff peaks.
6. Gently fold into the polenta mixture.
7. Tip into the cake tin and bake for 45 minutes, until it is golden and springs back when lightly touched (cover loosely with a sheet of foil if it browns too quickly).
8. Remove from the oven, leave in the tin and prick all over with a skewer.

Honey Syrup

1. Heat the syrup ingredients in a small pan until bubbling, then pour over the cake.
2. Allow to cool completely in the tin before removing.

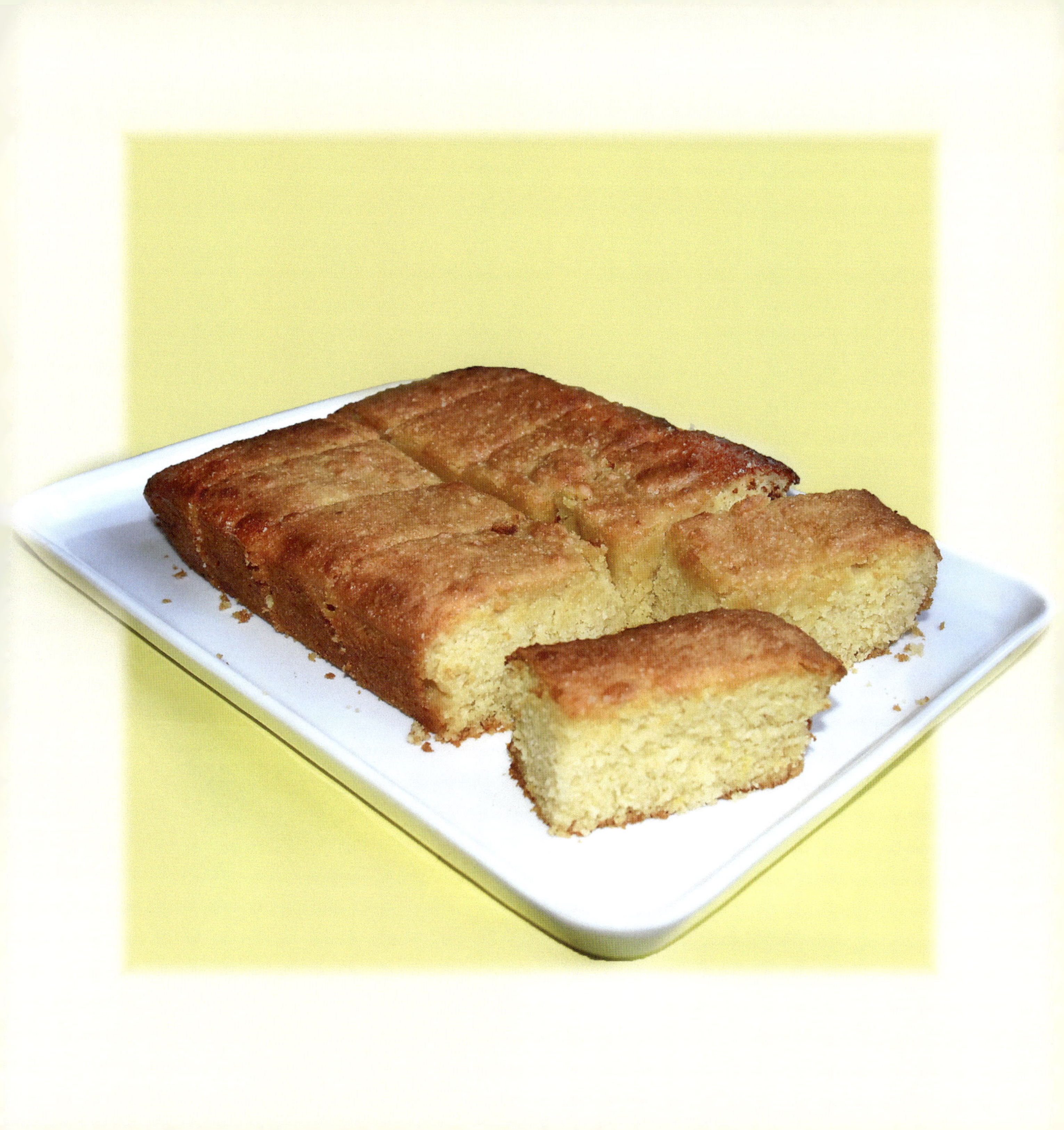

Meringue, Almond & Blackberry cake

Ingredients

Cake Ingredients
250g (1¼ cup) caster sugar
300g (1¼ cup) unsalted butter, softened
300g (2½ cup) self raising flour
40g (¼ cup) ground almonds
1 teaspoon almond essence
4 tablespoons milk
1 teaspoon baking powder
6 large eggs - 2 whole, 4 yolks - (the whites saved for the meringue)

200g (1½ cup) blackberries, roughly chopped

Meringue
4 egg whites
200g (1 cup) caster sugar
40g (½ cup) flaked almonds

NOTE: This cake can be tricky to cut into slices due to the crunchy meringue topping. Delicious served with whipped cream.

Method

1. Preheat the oven to 170°C / 325°F / gas 3
2. Line a 7x11ins (18x28cm) traybake tin with parchment paper
3. Place all the cake ingredients, except the blackberries, into a bowl and beat using an electric hand whisk until well blended
4. Spread the mixture evenly in the tin
5. Scatter the blackberries over the top.

Meringue
1. In a clean separate bowl whisk the egg whites until forming soft peaks
2. Gradually add the sugar whisking between each addition
3. When the meringue is glossy and stiff, spread on the cake mixture
4. Sprinkle with the almonds
5. Bake for 1½ hours then reduce the oven temperature to 150°C, 300°F, gas 2 and bake for 30mins.
6. Switch the oven off and leave the cake in the oven to cool.

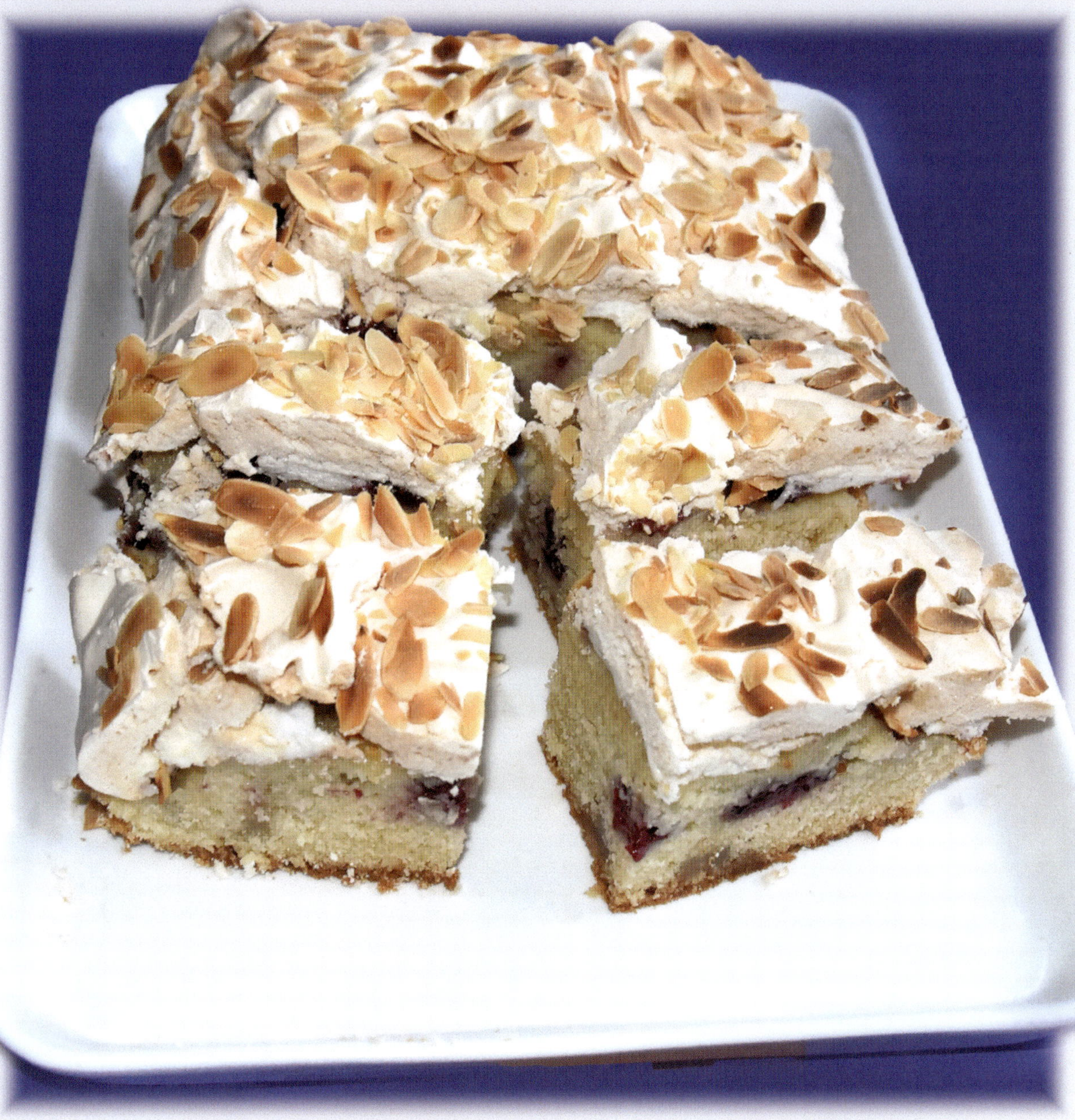

Millionaires Shortbread

Ingredients

Shortbread layer
250g (2 cups) plain flour
75g (½ cup) caster sugar
175g (¾ cup) softened butter

Caramel filling
100g (½ cup) butter
100g (½ cup) light muscovado sugar
2 x 397g cans (2½ cups) condensed milk

Chocolate topping
150g (1 cup) plain chocolate
50g (¼ cup) white chocolate

Method

1. Preheat the oven to 180°C / gas 4 / 350°F
2. Line a 7 x 11ins (18 x 28cm) traybake tin with parchment paper

Shortbread
1. Place all the shortbread ingredients in a bowl.
2. Rub the butter in with fingertips until mixture makes breadcrumbs, then knead to form a dough.
3. Press the dough into the tin, prick with a fork
4. Bake for 30 minutes until very lightly brown
5. Leave to cool in the tin

Caramel filling
1. Place all the caramel ingredients in a pan and heat gently until the sugar has dissolved
2. Bring to the boil stirring all the time then reduce the heat
3. Simmer gently for 5 minutes, stirring to ensure the mixture does not burn on the bottom
4. When the mixture has thickened to a soft fudge consistency pour over the shortbread and leave to cool in the fridge.

Chocolate topping
Melt the two chocolates in separate bowls set over pans of hot water.
Spread the plain chocolate over the cooled set caramel then drop the white chocolate on top and use a skewer to marble the chocolate together. Set in a cool place.

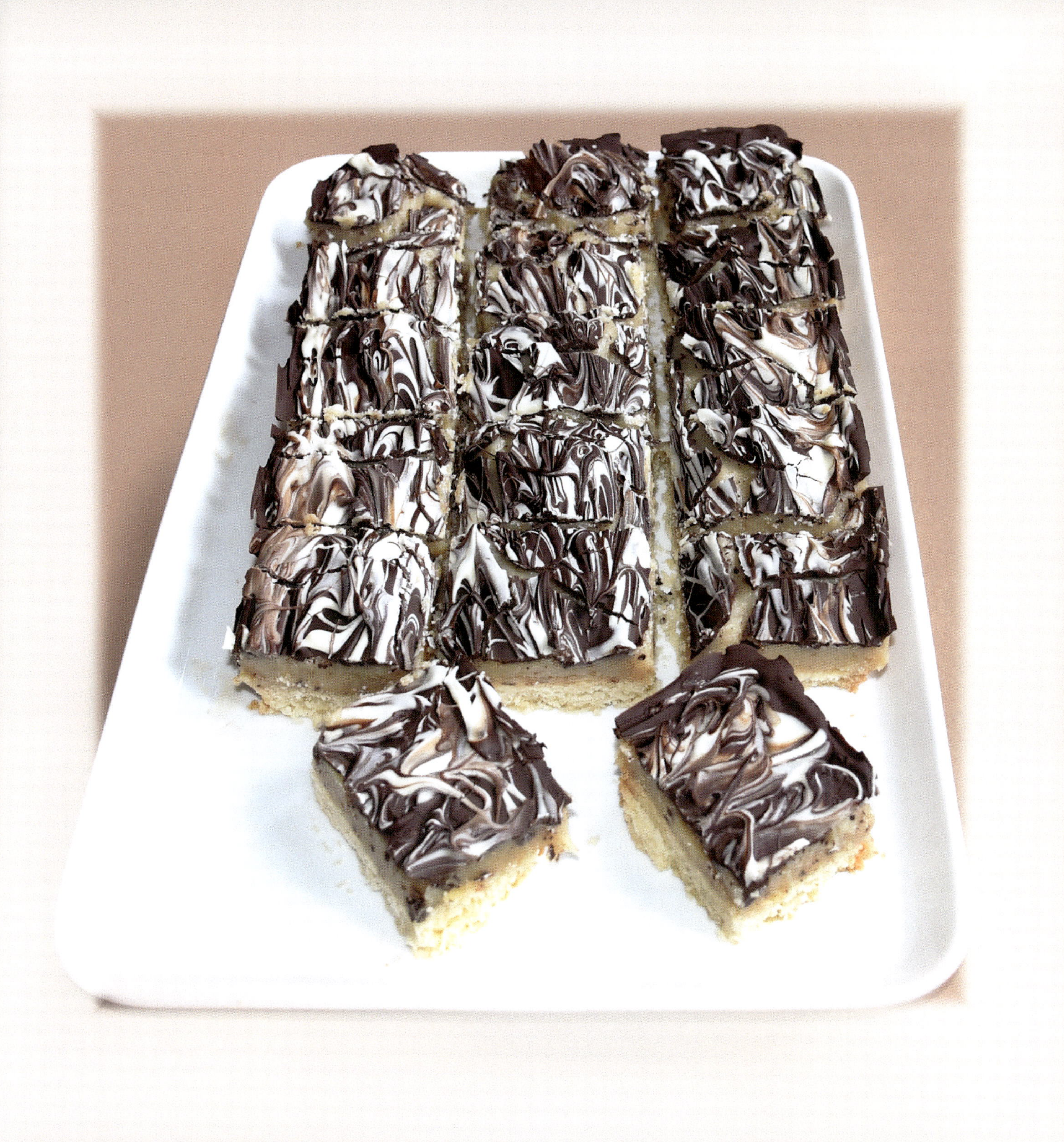

Peanut and Fudge Brownies

Ingredients

250g (1½ cup) plain dark chocolate
175g (¾ cup) unsalted butter
3 eggs
200g (1 cup) light muscovado sugar
80g (¾ cup) self raising flour
½ teaspoon baking powder
90g (½ cup) roasted salted peanuts, chopped
190g (½ cup) dairy fudge, roughly cut to 1cm pieces

Method

1. Preheat the oven to 190°C / 375°F / gas 5
2. Line a 7 x 11ins (18 x 28cm) traybake tin with parchment paper
3. Put the chocolate and butter in a bowl and melt, either using the microwave on medium power for 2-3 minutes or by resting the bowl over a pan of simmering water. Stir to make a smooth sauce.
4. In a separate bowl, whisk together the eggs and sugar until thick
5. Stir in the slightly cooled melted chocolate mixture
6. Then stir in the flour and baking powder
7. Lightly stir in half the fudge and nuts and turn into the tin, spreading the mixture evenly
8. Scatter with remaining fudge and nuts.
9. Bake in the oven for 30 minutes until a sugary crust has formed but the mixture feels wobbly underneath.
10. Leave to cool completely in the tin.

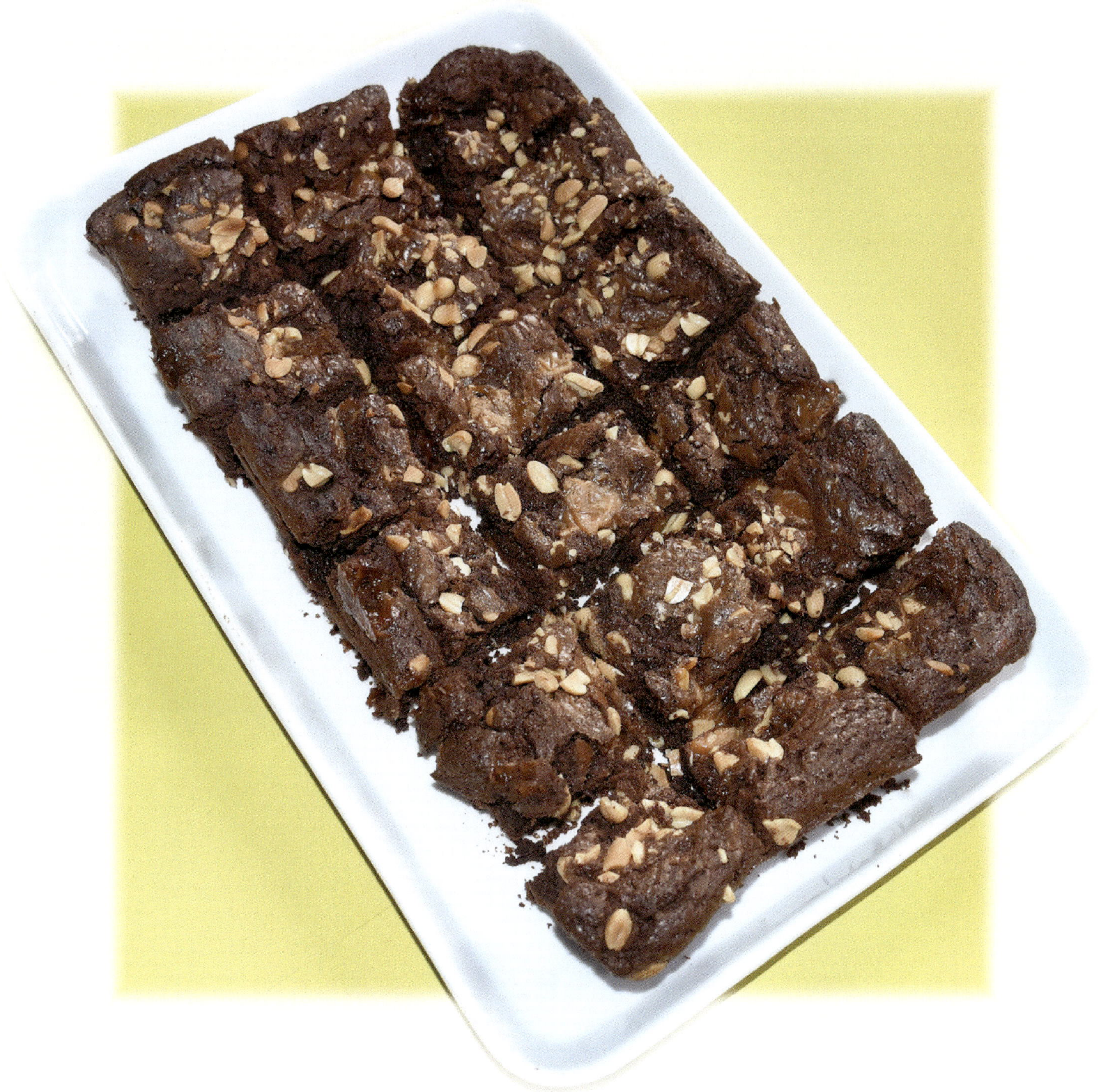

Peanut Butter Cake

Ingredients

300g (2½ cup) plain flour
2 teaspoons baking powder
½ teaspoon baking soda
½ teaspoon salt

5 tablespoons oil
100g (1/3 cup) smooth peanut butter
175g (1 cup) brown sugar
3 eggs
1 teaspoon vanilla extract

240ml (1 cup) buttermilk

Syrup
(¼ cup) honey
(¼ cup) brown sugar
2 tablespoons butter

Frosting
120g (½ cup) unsalted butter
120g (½ cup) peanut butter
6 tablespoons buttermilk
1 teaspoons vanilla extract
450g (3½ cups) confectioner's icing sugar

Cake Decoration (optional)

Method

1. Preheat the oven to 180°C / gas 4 / 350°F
2. Line a 7 x 11ins (18 x 28cm) traybake tin with parchment paper
3. Sift the flour, baking powder, baking soda and salt into a bowl and set aside
4. In a large mixing bowl beat the oil, peanut butter, sugar, eggs and vanilla until well combined
5. Add the dry ingredients to the peanut mixture in small batches alternating with the buttermilk and beat until just combined
6. Bake for 30 minutes until a skewer inserted into the middle comes out clean

Syrup
1. Put all the syrup ingredients in a saucepan and bring to a boil. Remove from heat.
2. Poke some holes in the cake and drizzle the syrup over.
3. Allow to cool, take out of the tin and cut in half horizontally

Frosting
1. Put the butter, peanut butter, buttermilk and vanilla in a saucepan and bring to the boil
2. Take off the heat and beat in the sugar.
3. Spread half the frosting on the bottom layer of the cake. Cover with the top cake layer and spread the rest of the frosting on top.

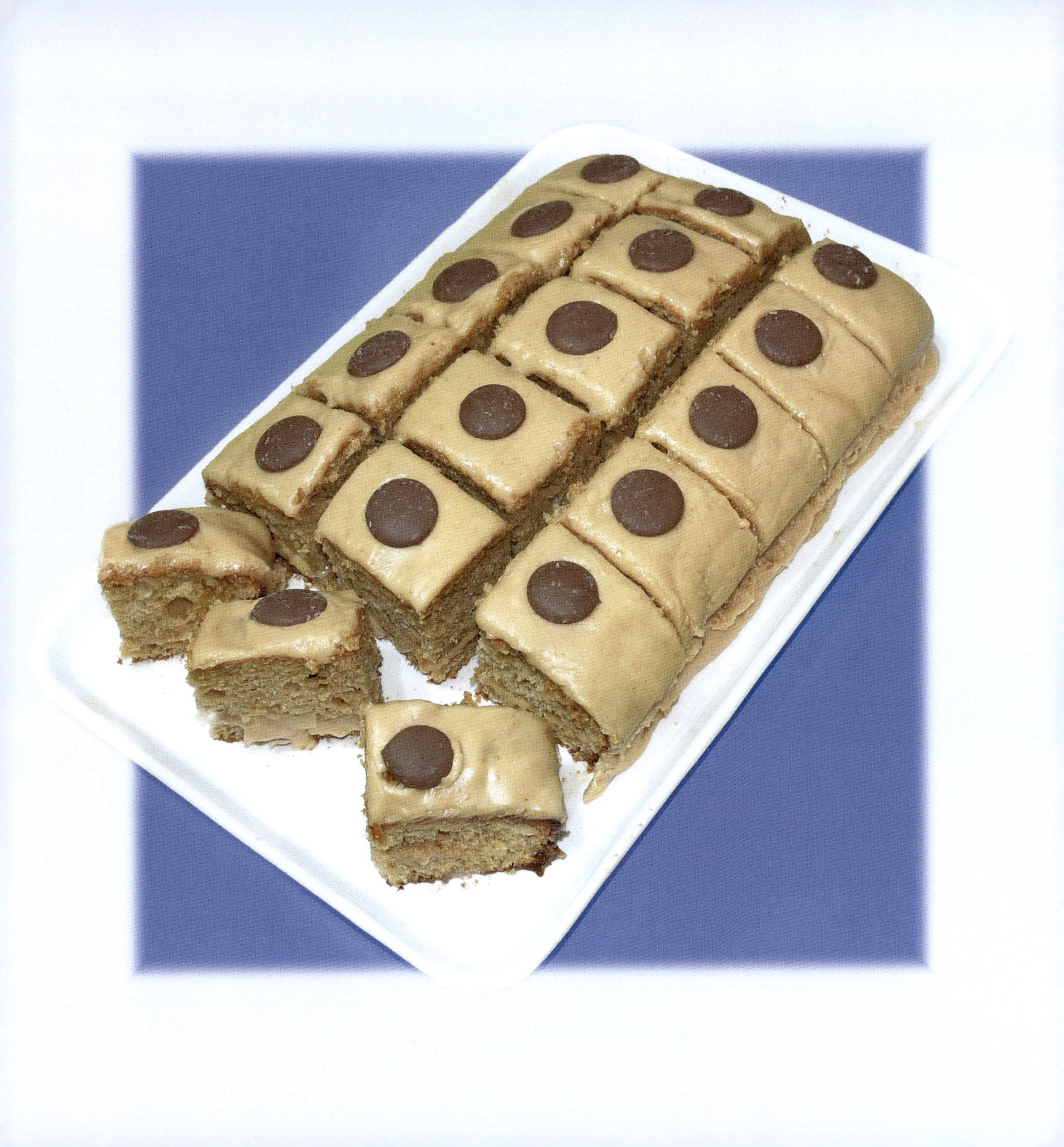

Pineapple Upside-Down cake

Ingredients

Topping

8 canned pineapple slices in juice (not syrup)
8 glace or maraschino cherries
60g (4 tablespoons) unsalted butter, melted
80g (½ cup) brown soft sugar

Cake
150g (¾ cup) softened butter
150g (¾ cup) light brown muscovado sugar
3 eggs
175g (1½ cup) self raising flour
1 teaspoon baking powder
pinch of salt

2 canned pineapple slices in juice (not syrup), finely chopped

Syrup
2 tablespoons pineapple juice
1 tablespoon lemon juice

Method

1. Preheat the oven to 180°C / gas 4 / 350°F
2. Line a 7 x 11ins (18 x 28cm) traybake tin with parchment paper

Topping
3. Pour the melted butter in the prepared tin
4. Sprinkle over the sugar
5. Dry the pineapple slices with a paper towel
6. Arrange on top of the sugar and decorate with the cherries
Press the fruit into the sugar

Cake
1. Place all the cake ingredients apart from the chopped pineapple in a large bowl
2. Using an electric hand whisk beat together until well combined
3. Stir in the chopped pineapple
4. Put the cake mixture on top of the pineapple in the tin and level the top
5. Bake for 25 minutes then lower the heat to 150°C/ 300°F/ gas 2 and bake for another 20 minutes.
6. Turn out on to a plate.

Syrup
Mix the pineapple and lemon juice together and spoon over the cake.

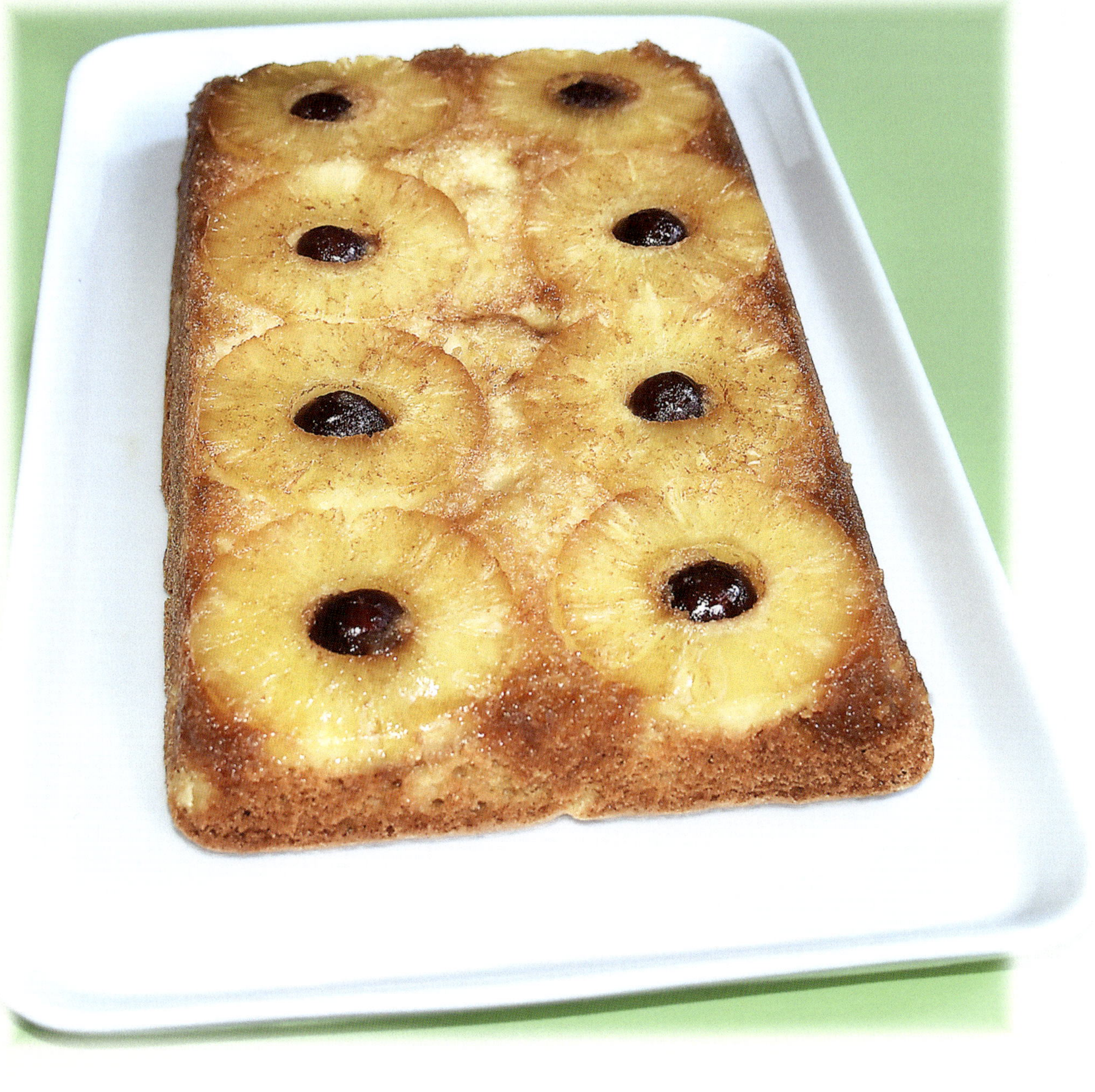

Raspberry Mousse Slices

Ingredients

Biscuit Base
250g (20 biscuits) bourbon biscuits
70g (¼ cup) butter

Raspberry Mousse

500g (4 cups) raspberries, fresh or frozen
100g (½ cup) caster sugar

400ml (1¾ cups) double cream
4 teaspoons gelatin

Jelly topping
275ml (½ pint, 1 cup) raspberry jelly made up to pack instructions

Method

Biscuit Base
1. Line a 7 x 11ins (18 x 28cm) traybake tin with parchment paper
2. Place the biscuits in a plastic bag and crush with a rolling pin to make crumbs
3. Melt the butter
4. Add the biscuit crumbs to the butter and stir to coat
5. Press the biscuit crumbs firmly into the base of the tin

Raspberry Mousse
1. Place the rasberries and sugar in a pan and heat gently until the sugar dissolves
2. Blend with a hand blender till smooth then strain through a sieve and discard the seeds
3. In a large bowl whisk the cream to soft peaks
4. Dissolve the gelatine in a little water and add to the raspberries
5. Immediately add the raspberry mixture to the cream and whisk in
6. Pour mousse onto the biscuit base and put in the fridge for 3 hours until set.

Jelly topping
Make up the jelly as on the pack instructions and allow to cool but not set.
Pour over the mousse and put back in the fridge to set.

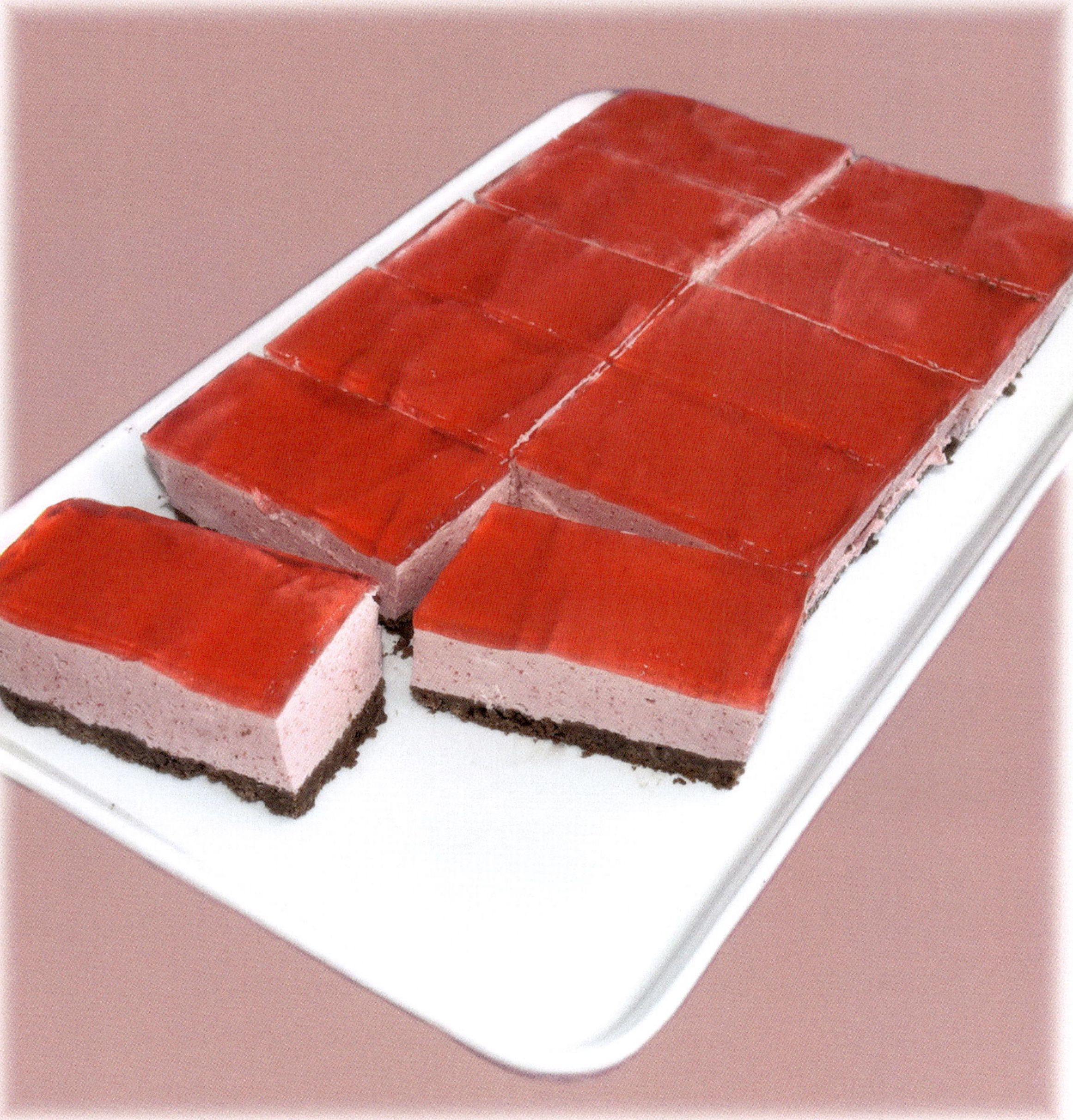

Sticky Apple Traybake

Ingredients

Sponge layer
250g (2 cups) self raising flour
75g (1/3 cup) soft brown sugar
50g (½ cup) ground almonds
115g (½ cup) butter, softened
2 egg yolks
1 tablespoons lemon juice

Filling
4 medium bramley cooking apples
115g (½ cup) soft brown sugar
1 tablespoons lemon juice

Topping
75g (½ cup) plain flour
200g (1 cup) soft brown sugar
2 teaspoons ground cinnamon
75g (¼ cup) butter

Method

1. Preheat the oven to 180°C / gas 4 / 350°F
2. Line a 7 x 11ins (18 x 28cm) traybake tin with parchment paper

Sponge layer
1. Put all the sponge layer ingredients in a bowl and using an electric hand whisk or food processor combine until well mixed.
2. Press into the tin.

Filling
1. Peel, core and slice the apples.
2. Combine with the sugar and lemon juice
3. Arrange over the sponge mixture

Topping
1. Place all the topping ingredients in a bowl and rub with finger tips to form crumbs.
2. Sprinkle over the apples.
3. Bake in the centre of the oven for 1 to 1¼ hours.
4. Turn off the oven and allow to cool in the oven
5. Turn out on a serving plate.

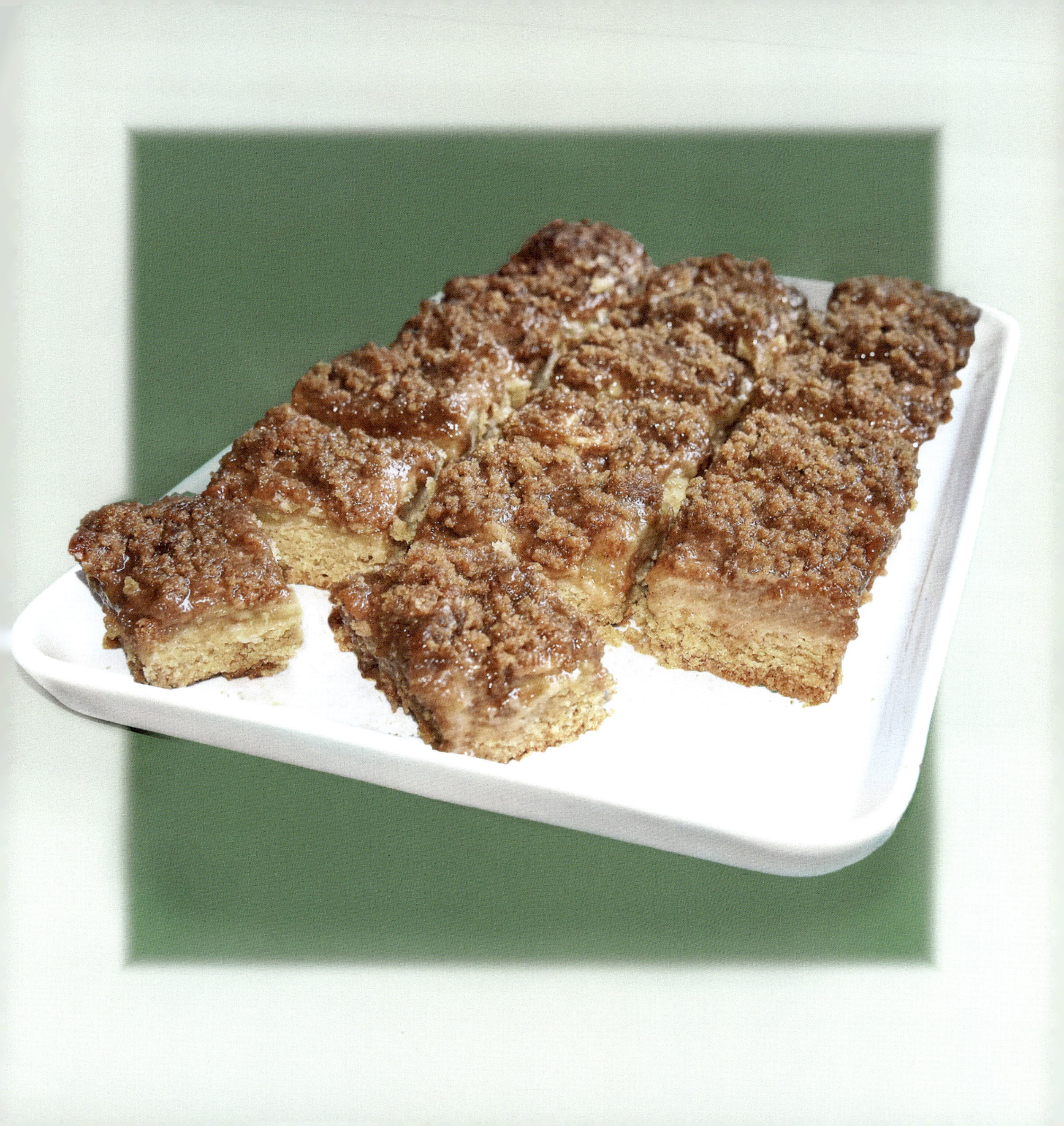

Stollen Squares

Ingredients

For the fruit
75g (½ cup) raisins
75g (½ cup) glacé cherries, halved
3 tablespoons lemon juice

Biscuit base
150g (¾ cup) butter
65g (¼ cup) caster sugar
225g (1¾ cups) plain flour

Cake layer
150g (¾ cup) butter, at room temperature
100g (½ cup) caster sugar
3 eggs, beaten
½ teaspoon almond extract
150g (1¼ cup) self-raising flour
225g (1 cup) marzipan/almond paste, coarsely grated

1 tablespoon icing sugar for sprinkling (optional)

Method

1. A few hours before baking (or the night before) soak the fruit in the lemon juice.
2. When ready to start baking, preheat the oven to 180°C / gas 4 / 350°F
3. Line a 7 x 11ins (18 x 28cm) traybake tin with parchment paper

Biscuit base
1. Cream the butter and sugar together until combined.
2. Work in the flour, then knead for a few seconds until smooth.
3. Press into the tin in an even layer, using the back of a spoon to smooth it down.
4. Bake for 20 minutes, then remove from the oven and leave to cool.

Cake layer
1. Beat the butter and sugar together until light and fluffy.
2. Gradually beat in the eggs and almond extract.
3. Fold in the flour using a large metal spoon.
4. Drain the fruit and stir into the mixture
5. Sprinkle the marzipan evenly over the biscuit base, then spoon the cake mixture on top.
6. Bake for 25-30 minutes, until evenly browned on the surface. Cool completely.
7. Sieve the icing sugar over the cake then remove from the tin and cut into squares

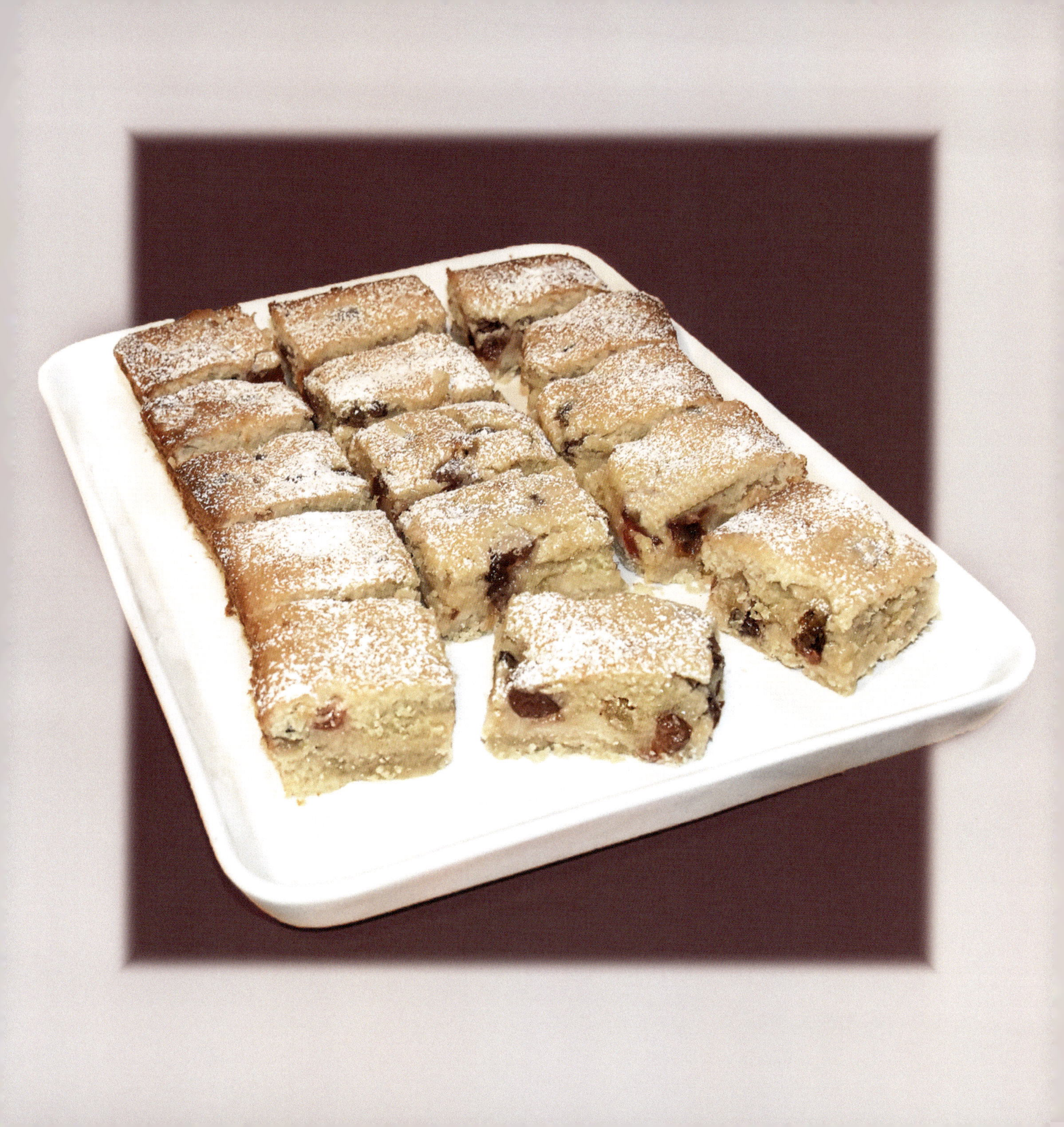

Summer Fruit Slices

Ingredients

190g (1½ cup) self-raising flour, sifted
125g (1¼ cup) ground almonds
220g (1 cup) unsalted butter, softened
150g (¾ cup) caster sugar
3 eggs

2 tablespoons milk
1 teaspoon almond or vanilla essence

475g (3 cups) frozen summer fruits, thawed and drained or fresh fruit

25g (¼ cup) granulated sugar

Method

1. Preheat the oven to 180°C / gas 4 / 350°F
2. Line a 7 x 11ins (18 x 28cm) traybake tin with parchment paper
3. Put the flour, almonds, butter, sugar and eggs in a bowl
4. Beat with an electric mixer to combine
5. Stir in the milk and almond essence
6. Then fold in 200g fruit.
7. Spoon into the tin and level the surface.
8. Scatter with the remaining fruit and bake for 50-60 minutes, until golden and firm, and a skewer comes out clean.
9. Scatter with the granulated sugar
10. Cool in the tin, then transfer to a wire rack.

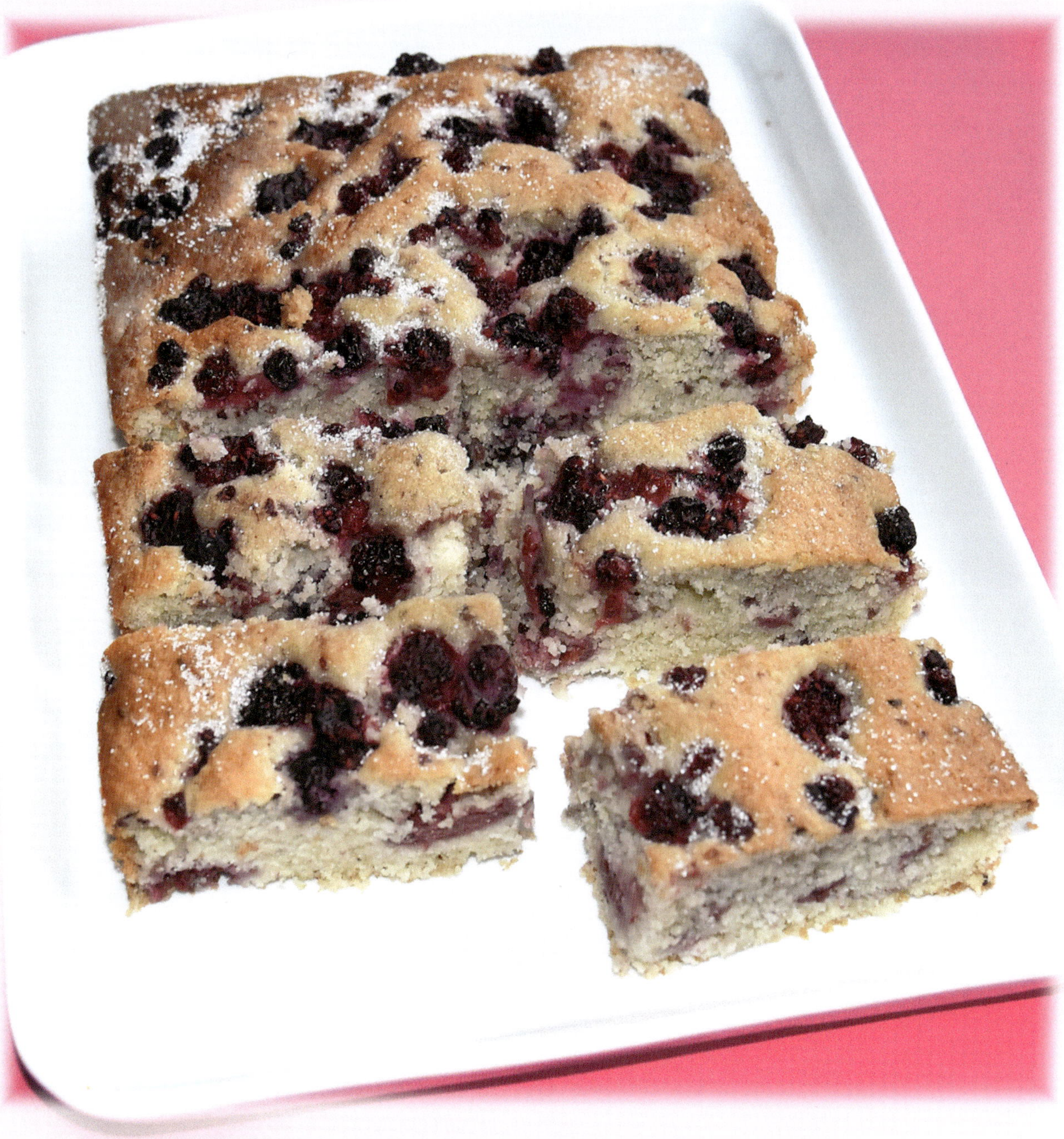

Tiramisu

Ingredients

Biscuit base
200g (2 cups) Amaretti biscuits, crushed
60g (1/3 cup) butter, melted

Filling
3 x 250g tubs (3 cups) mascarpone cheese
60g (½ cup) icing sugar

Coffee layer
3 tablespoons instant coffee
3 tablespoons brandy (optional)
15 tablespoons hot water
18 sponge fingers

Decoration
cocoa powder for dusting

Method

Biscuit base
1. Line a 7 x 11ins (18 x 28cm) traybake tin with parchment paper
2. Mix the amaretti biscuits with the melted butter
3. Press firmly into the base of the tin (use a potato masher for a firm flat surface)

Filling
1. Place the mascarpone and icing sugar in a bowl and mix together.
2. Spread 1/3 of the mixture over the base.

Coffee layer
1. In a shallow bowl mix the coffee, water and brandy if using.
2. Dip the sponge fingers in the coffee one at a time and letting them soak up the coffee.
3. Lay the sponge fingers on top of the mascarpone in an even layer
4. Top with the rest of the mascarpone mixture
5. Chill the tiramisu for at least 30 minutes or overnight before dusting with cocoa powder and serving

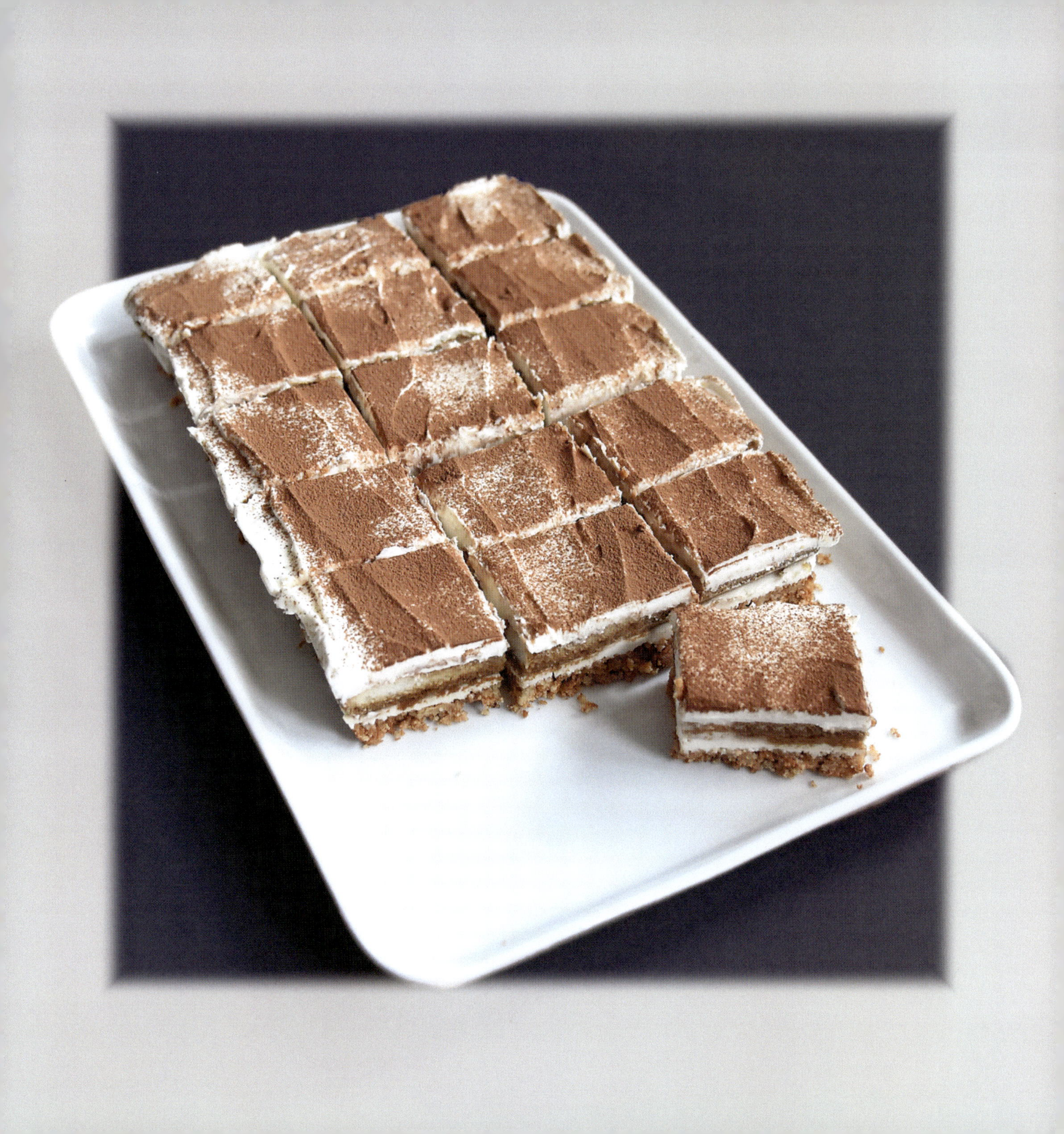

Toffee and Apple Flapjack Squares

Ingredients

175g (¾ cup) unsalted butter
50g (¼ cup) light brown muscovado sugar
3 tablespoons golden syrup
2 tablespoons black treacle
350g (4¼ cup) rolled/porridge oats

Filling
465g (1¾ cup) jar apple sauce

Topping
150g (1 cup or 20) dairy toffees
2 tablespoons milk

Method

1. Preheat the oven to 190°C / 375°F / gas 5
2. Line a 7 x 11ins (18 x 28cm) traybake tin with parchment paper
3. Place the butter, sugar, golden syrup, and treacle in a pan and heat gently until the butter has melted
4. Remove from the heat and stir in the oats
5. Place half the mixture in the tin and press down firmly with a spoon or a flat surface.
6. Spread the apple sauce over the base evenly.
7. Cover with the remaining flapjack mixture.
8. Bake for 30 minutes or until golden brown
9. Allow to cool in the tin

Topping
Put the toffees and milk in a small pan and heat gently until melted.
Drizzle the melted toffee over the flapjack and allow to cool completely
Cut into squares

NOTE: It's easier to cut the flapjacks with a serrated knife.
Alternately, the flapjacks could be removed from the tin when completely cooled, and cut into squares before the topping is drizzed over

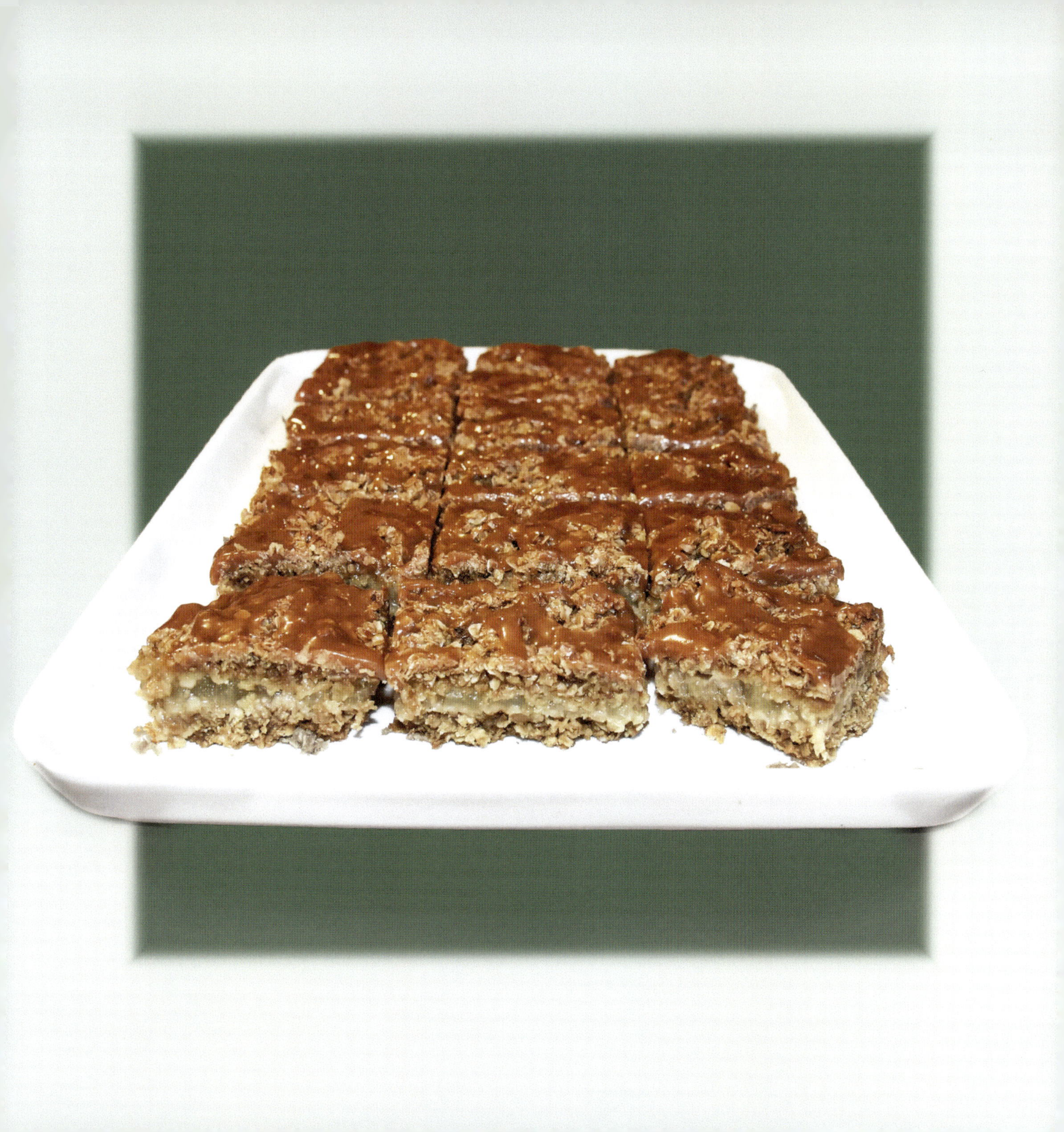

Vanilla Sponge

Ingredients

225g (1 cup) unsalted butter
200g (1 cup) caster sugar
1 teaspoon vanilla extract
3 eggs
250g (2 cups) self raising flour
1 teaspoon baking powder
¼ teaspoon salt
5 tablespoons milk

Vanilla Frosting

180g (¾ cup) unsalted butter, softened
375g (3 cups) icing sugar
6 tablespoons double/heavy cream
2 teaspoons vanilla extract

Decoration of your choice (optional)

Method

1. Preheat the oven to 180°C / 350°F / gas 4
2. Line a 7 x 11ins (18 x 28cm) traybake tin with parchment paper
3. In a large mixing bowl, use electric beaters to cream together the butter and sugar until light and fluffy.
4. Beat in the vanilla and eggs.
5. Gently add the flour, baking powder and salt until just combined
6. Stir in the milk
7. Tip the mixture into the tin and level the top
8. Bake for 30 minutes or until a skewer inserted into the middle comes out clean.
9. Set aside to cool in the tin.
10. When cool remove from the tin and slice in half.

Vanilla Frosting

1. To make frosting beat the butter with a hand held whisk until pale and creamy. This might take a few minutes.
2. Add the sugar a few spoonfuls at a time and beat in each addition
3. Beat in the cream and vanilla essence.
4. If the frosting is too thick add in extra cream or if its too thin add extra sugar.
5. Spread 1/3 of the frosting on the base of the cake then cover with the sponge top and spread the rest of the frosting on top.

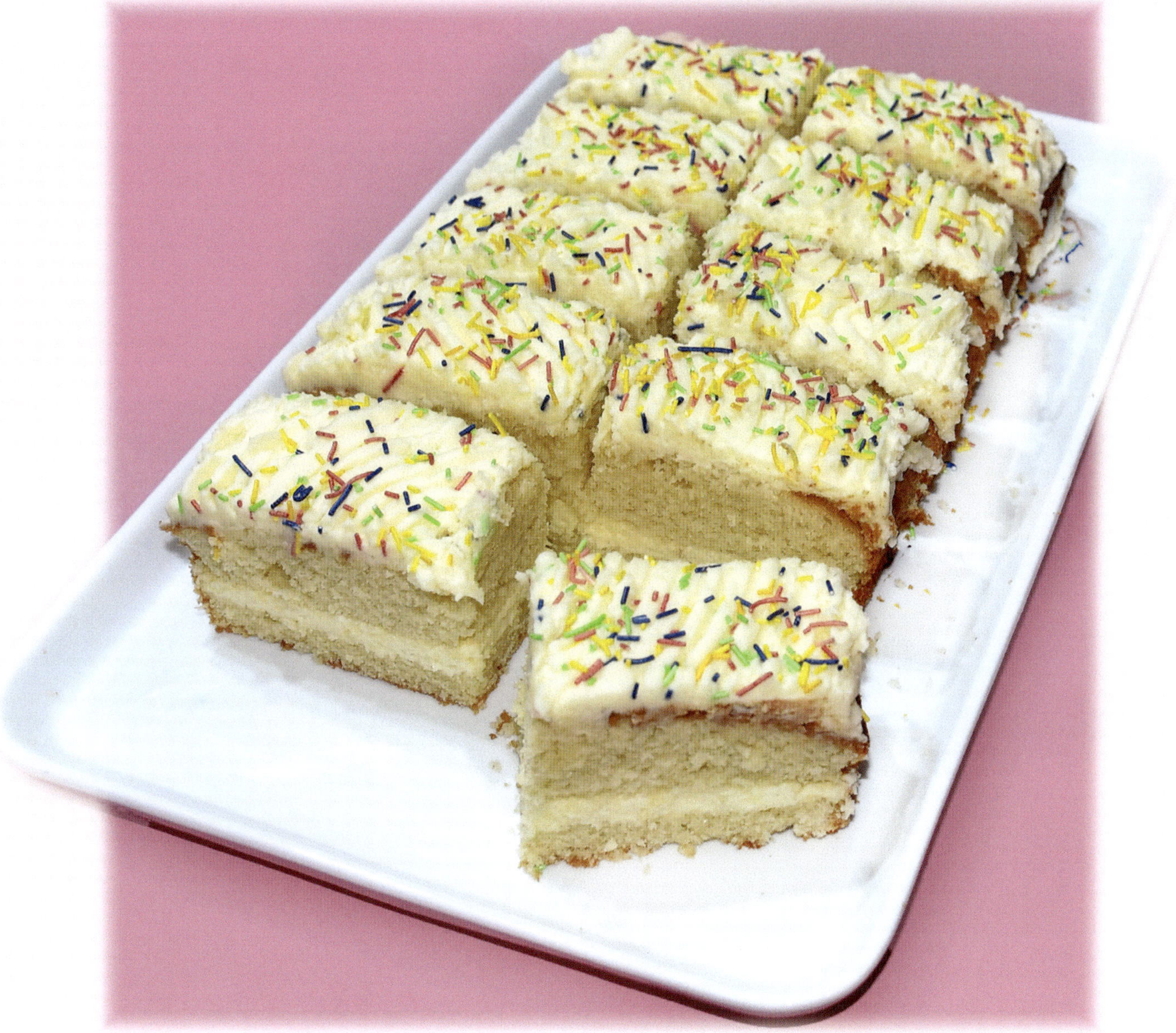

White Chocolate and Pecan Blondies

Ingredients

125g (¾ cup) pecans
190g (¾ cup) unsalted butter
150g (¾ cup) caster sugar
100g (½ cup) light brown muscovado sugar
3 eggs
2 teaspoons vanilla extract
160g (1¼ cup) plain flour
160g (1¼ cup) self raising flour
½ teaspoon salt
125g (¾ cup) white chocolate, roughly chopped

Decoration (optional)
45g (¼ cup) white chocolate

Method

1. Preheat the oven to 180°C / gas 4 / 350°F
2. Line a 7 x 11ins (18 x 28cm) traybake tin with parchment paper
3. Put the pecans on a baking tray and bake for 10 minutes. Set aside. When cooled down roughly chop.
4. Melt the butter and both sugars in a pan over a low heat stirring to combine. Allow to cool slightly
5. In a large bowl beat the eggs and vanilla
6. Whisk the butter and sugar mixture into the eggs
7. Beat in the flours and salt
8. Stir in the pecans and chocolate
9. Put into the tin and bake for 30 minutes until golden and a skewer inserted into the middle comes out clean
10. Allow to cool completely in the tin before removing

Decoration
Put the white chocolate in a bowl and melt over a pan of simmering water.
Drizzle over the cake.

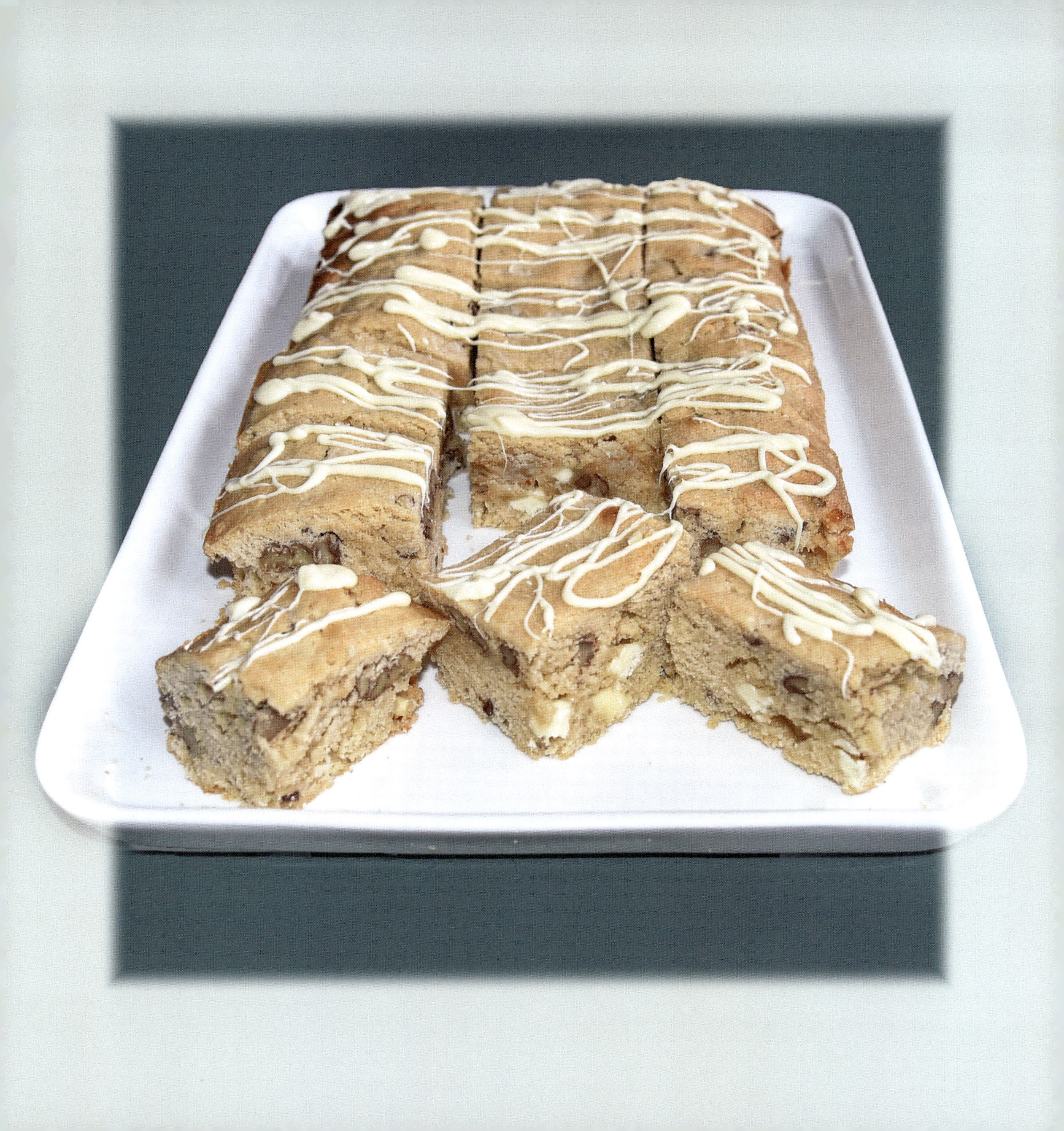

Whole Orange Cake

Ingredients

1 large orange, washed and cut into pieces (with the rind but seeds removed)

3 eggs
200g (1 cup) caster sugar
275g (2¼ cup) plain flour
2½ teaspoon baking powder
100g (½ cup) butter, softened
1 tablespoon vanilla extract
100g (½ cup) plain Greek yogurt

Icing
250g (2 cups) icing sugar
3 tablespoons milk

Decoration (optional)

Method

1. Preheat the oven to 180°C / gas 4 / 350°F
2. Line a 7 x 11ins (18 x 28cm) traybake tin with parchment paper
3. In a food processor or with an electric hand blender, process the whole orange until it is pureed.
4. In a separate bowl whisk the eggs and sugar until light and fluffy
5. Sift the flour and baking powder into a separate bowl
6. Add the flour to the mixture a little at a time along with the butter and continue to whisk until blended
7. Stir in the yogurt, vanilla and pureed orange
8. Put the batter in the tin and bake for 35 minutes or until a skewer comes out clean
9. Allow to cool before removing from the tin

Icing
When the cake is cooled sift the icing sugar into a bowl and mix in the milk.
Drizzle and spread over the cake and allow to set.

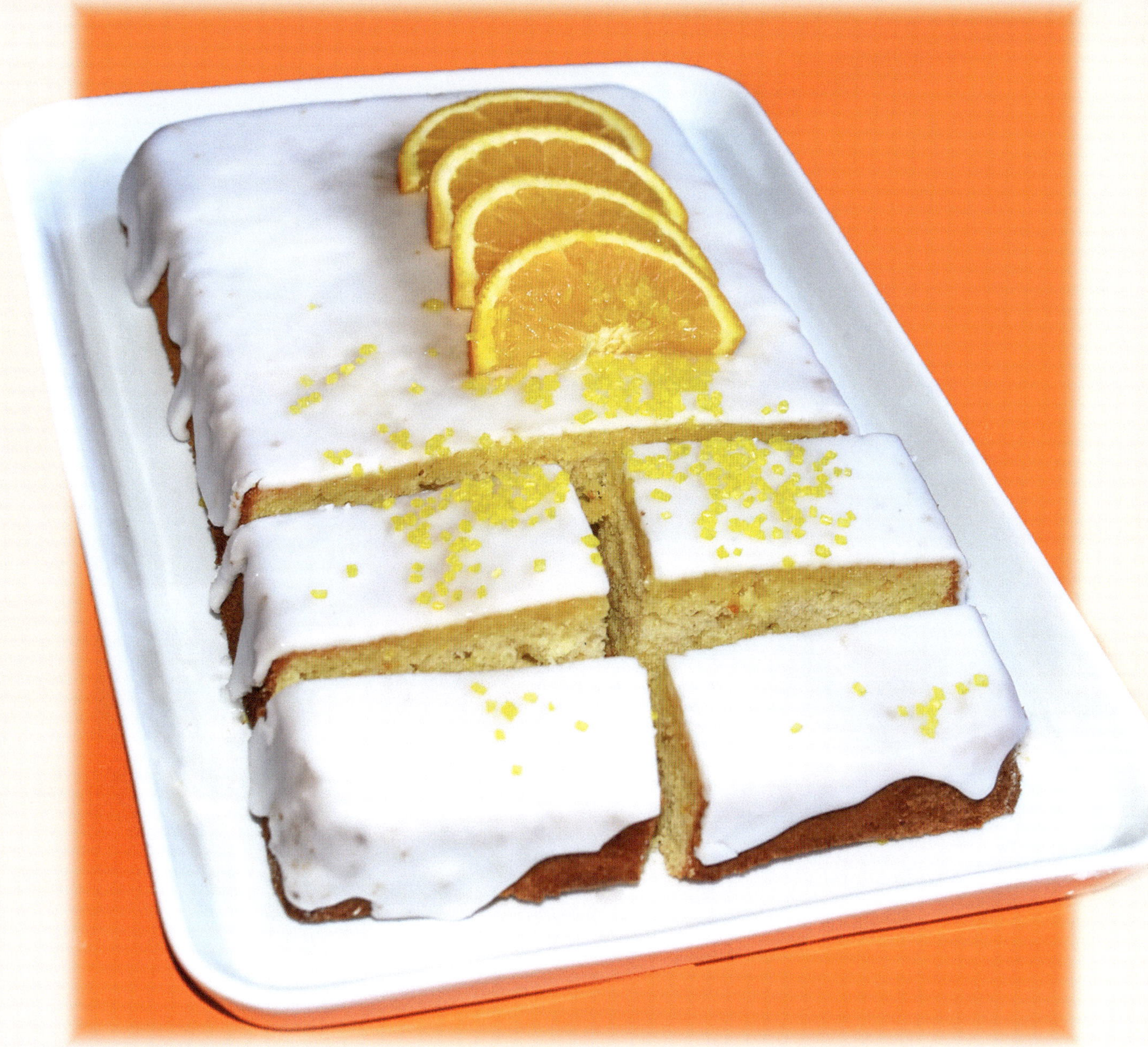

Printed in Great Britain
by Amazon